THE BASEBALL HANDBOOK
FOR COACHES AND PLAYERS

THE BASEBALL HANDBOOK FOR COACHES AND PLAYERS

Jim Depel

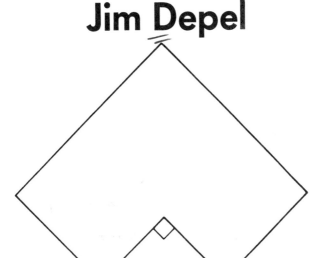

Collier Books
Macmillan Publishing Company • New York

Collier Macmillan Canada   Toronto

Maxwell Macmillan International
New York   Oxford   Singapore   Sydney

Collier Books
Macmillan Publishing Company
866 Third Avenue, New York, NY 10022

Collier Macmillan Canada, Inc.
1200 Eglinton Avenue East, Suite 200
Don Mills, Ontario M3C 3N1

Library of Congress Cataloging-in-Publication Data
Depel, Jim.
    The baseball handbook for coaches and players/
by Jim Depel.—1st Collier Books ed.
        p.   cm.
    Reprint. Originally published: New York : Scribner,
c1976.
    Includes index.
    ISBN 0-02-042861-8
    1. Baseball—Handbooks, manuals, etc.
2. Baseball—Coaching—Handbooks, manuals, etc.
I. Title.
    GV867.D4   1991   90–27450 CIP
    796.357'2—dc20

Macmillan books are available at special discounts for
bulk purchases for sales promotions, premiums,
fund-raising, or educational use.
For details, contact:

Special Sales Director
Macmillan Publishing Company
866 Third Avenue
New York, NY 10022

First Collier Books Edition 1991
10 9 8 7 6 5 4 3 2 1
Printed in the United States of America

CONTENTS

OFFENSE

HITTING AND BUNTING

HITTING

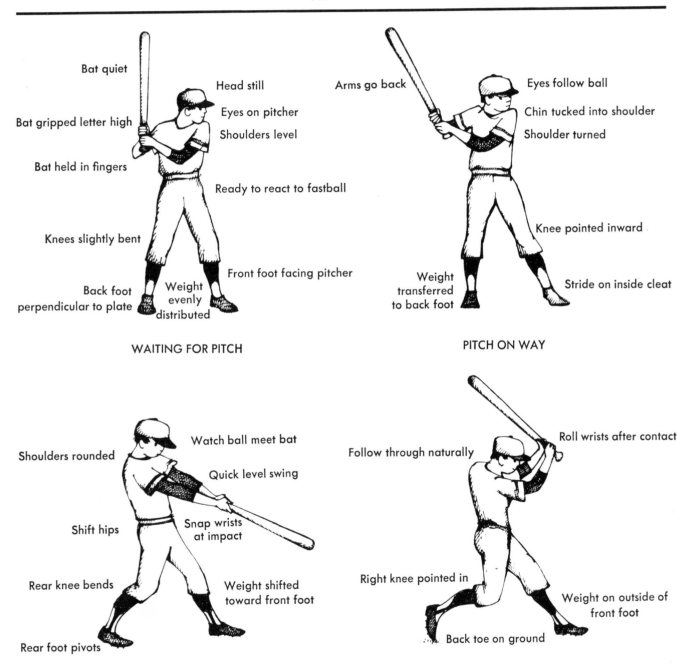

Bat quiet

Bat gripped letter high

Bat held in fingers

Knees slightly bent

Back foot perpendicular to plate

Head still

Eyes on pitcher

Shoulders level

Ready to react to fastball

Front foot facing pitcher

Weight evenly distributed

WAITING FOR PITCH

Arms go back

Eyes follow ball

Chin tucked into shoulder

Shoulder turned

Knee pointed inward

Weight transferred to back foot

Stride on inside cleat

PITCH ON WAY

Shoulders rounded

Watch ball meet bat

Quick level swing

Shift hips

Snap wrists at impact

Rear knee bends

Weight shifted toward front foot

Rear foot pivots

THE SWING

Follow through naturally

Roll wrists after contact

Right knee pointed in

Weight on outside of front foot

Back toe on ground

THE FOLLOW-THROUGH

FAULTS	CURES
Hitching	Raise back elbow—Hold hands still
Turning the Head	Point front shoulder toward pitcher—Keep eyes on ball—Don't swing so hard
Overstriding	Widen stance—Shorten stride—Put more weight on rear foot
Stepping in the Bucket	Shorten stride—Turn hips slightly inward—Overcome fear of being hit
Lunging	Put more weight on back foot—Bend back leg slightly—Turn hips slightly inward
Chopping	Raise front shoulder—Drop rear elbow—Put more weight on back foot
Uppercutting	Hold bat higher—Widen stance—Put more weight on front foot—Don't dip back knee—Raise back elbow
Difficulty Hitting the Change-Up	Turn hips slightly inward—Put more weight on rear foot—Delay swing—Hit to opposite field
Difficulty Hitting Curves Breaking Away	Turn hips slightly inward—Follow ball to bat—Delay swing—Hit to opposite field
Swinging at Bad Pitches	Know the strike zone

Position of baseball indicates if ball is hit out front or farther back

RIGHT-HANDED BATTER

Inside Pitch—Pull to left field   Middle Pitch—Hit straightaway   Outside Pitch—Hit to opposite field

SLUMPS

Reasons for Slumps

Faults in techniques
Eyes off ball
Timing (Increase daily batting practice)
Guessing with pitcher (Always be prepared for fastball)
Swinging too hard (Meet ball, don't kill it)
Injury
Fatigue
Excess weight on hips
Emotionally upset
Lack of confidence

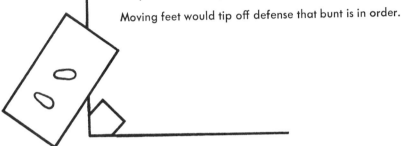

As pitcher's striding foot is about to hit ground, shift weight to front foot by rotating hips and bending knees slightly.

Keep feet stationary.

Moving feet would tip off defense that bunt is in order.

STANCE

"V" GRIP

The top hand grip is made with the thumb and the first two or three fingers, the thumb and the first finger forming a "V".

Bottom hand—Firm.

Top hand—Loose "V" grip.
  Slide top hand up as you rotate hips.
  Hit upper part of ball to avoid pop-up.
  "V" will absorb force of ball, preventing it from rolling too far.

HAND GRIP

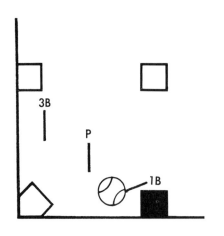

RUNNER ON 1ST BASE VS. RIGHT-HANDED 1ST BASEMAN

Bunt ball to 1st baseman.

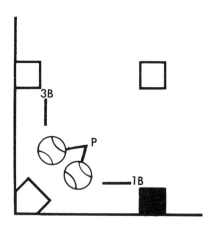

RUNNER ON 1ST BASE VS. LEFT-HANDED 1ST BASEMAN

Bunt ball to pitcher.

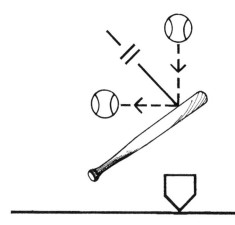

It's important to know that injection angle will be equal to reflection angle.

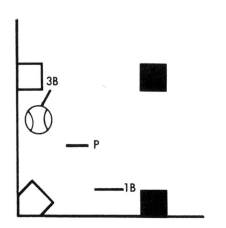

RUNNERS ON 1ST AND 2ND BASE

Bunt ball to 3rd baseman, forcing him to leave base and field ball.

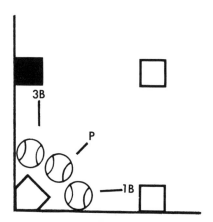

RUNNER ON 3RD BASE (SQUEEZE BUNT)

Doesn't matter where it's bunted as long as it's on ground.

BASERUNNING AND SLIDING TECHNIQUES

BASERUNNING

Leaving Batter's Box	Left-handed batters step out with the left foot first. Right-handed batters step out with the right foot first.
Rounding 1st Base	Run slightly to the right of the foul line the last half of the distance to 1st base (see page 71). Don't take too wide a turn in foul territory while rounding 1st base—it adds distance and time.
Rounding Any Base	Touch the inside corner of the base with the left foot: However, rather than break stride, it's better to use the right foot.
Stance on Base	Stand with the left foot on the base while looking at the coach for the sign.
Lead off Base	Weight on the balls of the feet, distributed evenly. Body slightly crouched. Knees bent slightly. Hands off the knees. Eyes focused on the pitcher.
Breaking for Next Base	Use cross-over step, left foot over right.
Tagging Up on Fly Balls	Crouch slightly, with one foot on the base, the other foot in line of the base you're going to. Keep eyes on the outfielder. Make a fake toward the next base, even if you have no intention of going, to try to draw a bad throw.
Runner on 3rd Base	Keep your feet outside the baseline. If base runner is hit by batted ball while he is in fair territory, he is out.

SLIDING TECHNIQUES

General	Be aware of which side of the base the throw is on. Start the slide about 8 to 10 feet before reaching the base. Once you decide to slide, go through with it, in order not to catch your cleats in the dirt. Keep your eyes on the base throughout the slide. Keep your arms and hands raised off the ground.
Feetfirst Slide	*Purpose: To beat the throw on a force play* Fall to either side. Slide on the hip and the side of the back. Extend both legs.

Hook Slide
Purpose: To avoid the tag

You may hook to either side. Learn both.

If hooking to the right side, take off on the left foot; the body falls to the right side, with the right hip and thigh absorbing the fall.

Both legs should be extended, and the toes should be pointed.

The left toe catches the outer edge of the base.

The body slides to the right side of the base in a flat position.

If the left leg is bent rather than extended, you travel a longer distance (referred to as the 93-foot slide).

Bent-Leg Slide
Purpose: To slow down by sliding and to rise quickly to be able to go to the next base (when no play is being made on you, or the ball is thrown wild, and you're going too fast to stand up)

Take off on either leg.

One leg is extended, other leg is bent.

The weight is absorbed on the outer side of the lower bent leg.

The foot of the extended leg catches the base, and the body momentum plus the straightening of the bent leg enables the runner to stand.

Headfirst Slide
This is a dangerous slide, and you should not use it except in getting back to a base, as in a pickoff attempt. Even then, be hesitant about using it.

Breaking Up a Double Play
Although it is legal to break up a double play by sliding into the baseman (provided you don't slide more than 3 feet to either side of the base and you don't raise your hands to interfere with the throw), safety should be considered for the baseman as well as yourself.

DEFENSE

DEFENSIVE POSITIONS

PITCHING

Conditioning	Keep your legs in good shape. As you get older and less active, you should do more jogging.
	Start the season by getting the arm in shape slowly. Take about 10 days before you start throwing full speed.
	Warm up well before each practice. Take a little longer on cold days.
Grip	Grip the ball on the seams, using the grip that you like best.
	Hold the ball firmly, but not tightly.
	The three pressure points are the index and middle fingers and the thumb.
Stance—With No Runners on Base	*The right-handed pitcher getting the catcher's signal*
	The front cleat of the pivot foot should be just over the front edge of the pitching rubber.
	The weight is on the left foot, which is slightly back of the right foot.
	The body should be relaxed.
	The eyes should be on the target and should stay there throughout the delivery.
Delivery—With No Runners on Base	As the arms go back, the weight is shifted to the front (right) foot.
	As the arms swing forward and up over the head, the weight is shifted back to the left foot.
	At the top, the weight is shifted back to the right foot.
	With the left leg bent, don't kick too high.
	Twist back as far as natural.
	In striding, step out straight ahead with the left foot, as if walking off the mound.
	Stride out a comfortable distance. Stepping too far to the right with the left foot causes you to throw across your body, which prevents you from following through and, therefore, getting the most out of your pitch.
Stance—With Runners on Base	*The right-handed pitcher getting the catcher's signal*
	The outer edge of the right foot should be just over the front edge of the pitcher's rubber.
	The left foot is a comfortable distance in front of the pitcher's rubber.
Stretch—With Runners on Base	As the hands go up and meet over the head, take a short stride with the left foot.
	As the hands come down, the left foot is brought back in.
	The hands meet at the hips for one count.
	The weight is evenly balanced after the stretch.
	When checking on a base runner at 1st base, if your left foot remains opened about 45° before and after the stretch, this will point your shoulder slightly toward 1st base and allow you to check on the base runner without moving your shoulders. Moving the shoulder is a balk.

17

Pitches	*A ball will break in the direction of its rotation*
	Rotation up—Fastball.
	Rotation left—Curve (right-handed pitcher).
	Rotation right—Screwball (right-handed pitcher).
	Rotation down—Drop.
	Change-Up
	Place the ball farther back in the palm, with the fingertips raised off the ball.
	Throw with the same motion as the fastball, except do not break the wrist.
	Release the ball by raising the fingers, not letting the ball spin off the fingertips.
	Drag the pivot foot to slow down the speed of the shoulder and arm and, consequently, the ball.
	Never throw a change-up
	To a weak hitter.
	To a choke hitter.
	To an opposite-field hitter.
	To a batter with his weight on the back foot.
	Above the batter's waist.
Reasons for Poor Control	Striding too far to the right with the left foot (right-handed pitcher).
	Overstriding—Will cause ball to go high.
	Understriding—Will cause ball to go low.
	Not following through.
	Poor physical condition.
	Pitching too many innings without rest.
	Psychological—Worry, fear, and so forth.
Fielding	On any ground ball hit to your left, break for 1st base.
	Aim for a point about 20 to 25 feet to the home-plate side of 1st base, then curve just inside the baseline toward the base, catching the ball on the run, and tagging the base with the right foot.
	When backing up bases, do so by about 35 feet.

CATCHING

Stance While Giving Sign	Squat position.
	Feet comfortable distance apart.
	The right knee pointed at the pitcher in order to hide the sign from the 1st-base coach.
	The left forearm on the thigh. The catcher's mitt hides the sign from the 3rd-base coach.
Stance After Giving Sign	Rise up somewhat from the squat position and take a comfortable stance as close as possible to the batter.
	Feet spread apart.
	Right foot slightly behind the left for good balance.
	Throwing hand relaxed, with the fingers closed loosely.
	Hold target still until the pitch is thrown.

Throwing to Bases	Take one step and throw. For every step you take, the base runner is taking a stride closer to the base.
Tagging Out Base Runner	You can block home plate *only* if you have the ball. Hold the ball in the bare hand and cover it with the mitt. Tag the runner with the back side of the catcher's mitt.
Bunts	Assist the fielders by giving directions for throws on bunts.
Pop Flies	If the pop-up is near the plate, hold the mask in the bare hand until you know for sure where the ball will land; then toss the mask away. This will prevent you from tripping on it. Any pop fly behind home plate will drift slightly toward the infield due to the rotation of the ball.
Wild Pitch—Runner on 3rd Base	As you are going after the ball, the pitcher will direct you to hold or to throw the ball. If throwing: Pick up the ball, with your left shoulder pointing toward home plate. This prevents having to shuffle your feet. Without rising, flip the ball underhanded to the pitcher, who is covering home plate.

INFIELD

Playing Conditions	Hard infield—The ball will move fast and bounce high. Wet infield—The ball will stay low. Wind—You can test the wind by checking the foul-line flags or by tossing grass into the air.
Knowing the Batter	Know his speed. It determines how deep you play and how fast you charge the ball. Know where the batter usually hits the ball.
Knowing the Situation	Before each pitch, know: Number of outs. If there are any base runners. If it's a bunt situation. If it's a steal situation. Know what you are going to do if it's a: Bunt. Ground ball. Line drive to you, if runners are on base. Single. Extra-base hit.

Stance	The toes should point slightly outward.
	The knees should be bent slightly.
	The weight should be distributed evenly on the balls of the feet.
	The hands should hang down inside the legs, with the palm of the glove facing the batter.
	On each pitch, rock forward slightly.
Fielding	Use the cross-over step. If the ball is hit to your left, step first with the right foot. If the ball is hit to your right, step first with the left foot.
	Get directly in front of the bouncing ball.
	Play the hop, either the *short* hop or the *high* hop.
	Short Hop—Just as the ball comes off the ground.
	High Hop—At the peak of the hop.
	The eyes should be on the ball.
	The legs should be spread.
	The knees should be bent.
	The buttocks should be low.
	The hands should be relaxed and away from the body.
	The hands give slightly as the ball enters the glove.
	Don't hitch, that is, don't drop the hands or bring them near the body prior to the throw.
	Use as little time as possible in fielding the ball.
Throwing	Throw the ball about letter high. Look where you are throwing.
	Take only one step before you throw.
	Use a snap throw. It saves time.
	Follow through.
Pop Flies	The player coming in on the ball should make the catch. He can judge the ball best.
	Fly balls between the catcher and the infielder should be caught by the infielder.
	Fly balls between the infielder and the outfielder should be caught by the outfielder.
Tagging Out a Base Runner	Straddle the base.
	Lay the glove down in front of the base, the back side of the glove facing the base runner.
	Let the base runner slide into the glove.
	Keep the bare hand out of the way.
Rundown Play	*Runner caught off 1st base*
	The 1st baseman chases the base runner toward 2nd base.
	When the base runner gets halfway to 2nd base, the 1st baseman throws the ball to the shortstop, who is covering 2nd base.
	The 1st baseman passes the base runner on the glove-hand side and continues on to cover 2nd base.
	The shortstop chases the runner back toward 1st base, faking a throw to 1st base, hoping to get the base runner to stop for a tag out.
	If the runner does not stop, he tosses the ball to the 2nd baseman, who is covering 1st base, for the putout. The shortstop continues on toward 1st base. The cycle continues if the base runner reverses his direction.
	The putout should be made at the base from which the runner left, with as few throws as possible.

Appeal Play	Always check to see if a base runner tags all of the bases. If not, call for the ball and tag either the base or the base runner. Then make the appeal to the umpire. The umpire cannot call the base runner out unless you make the appeal, even though he may see the runner miss the base.

1ST BASE

Holding a Runner on 1st Base	The heel of the right foot is near the inner edge of the corner of the base nearest the pitcher. The left foot is near the 1st base foul line.
Tagging Base Runner on Pickoff Attempt	Use a sweeping motion.
Expecting a Bunt	*With a runner on 1st base only* Keep base runner close. After the pitch, rush toward the batter. *With runners on 1st and 2nd base* Play far in on the infield.
Catching the Ball	*Shift method* Straddle the base. Place the heel of your left foot against the home-plate side of the base. Place the heel of your right foot against the 2nd-base side of the base. If the ball is thrown to your left, take a hop to your left, placing the toe of your right foot where your left heel was. Stretch. If the ball is thrown to your right, take a hop to your right, placing the toe of your left foot where your right heel was. Stretch. On high throws, don't jump unless it's impossible to catch the ball otherwise.
Pitcher Covering 1st Base	*Close to 1st base* Toss the ball to the pitcher a couple of strides before he reaches the base. Lead him by tossing the ball slightly in front of him. Toss the ball underhanded, about face high. *Far from 1st base* Throw the ball overhanded.

2ND BASE

On a Steal	Cover the base when there is a right-handed batter.
Expecting a Bunt	Play a little closer toward 1st base.
Throwing the Ball on a Double Play	*Short distance* Toss the ball underhanded, about face high.

Medium distance (10 to 15 feet away)
Use a counterclockwise twist of the wrist, and flip the ball with the back of the hand facing you.

Long distance
Use hip-pivot, and sidearm the ball.

Approaching the Base on a Double Play	Start toward the base fast. Two or three strides before reaching the base, slow up and get under control.
Receiving the Ball on a Double Play	*Easiest method for beginners* Step on the right-field side of 2nd base with the left foot. Receive the throw. Transfer your weight to the right foot. Step to the outer side of the diamond and toward 1st base with the left foot. Throw.
Extra-Base Hits	To left field and center field—Cover 2nd base, and direct the relay. To right field—You're the relay man.

SHORTSTOP

Covering 2nd Base on a Steal	Cover the base when there's a left-handed batter.
Bunt Situation—Runner on 2nd Base	Hold the runner close to 2nd base.
Throwing the Ball on a Double Play	*Short distance* Toss the ball underhanded, about face high. *Medium or long distance* Throw the ball sidearm or overhanded. Don't hurry your throw. The lead runner is the most important to get out.
Approaching 2nd Base on a Double Play	Start toward the base fast. Two or three strides before reaching the base, slow up and get under control.
Receiving the Ball on a Double Play	*Easiest method for beginners* With your right foot in the baseline between 2nd and 3rd base, step on the 3rd-base side of 2nd base with your left foot. Receive the throw. Transfer your weight to your right foot. Step to the inner side of the diamond and toward 1st base with the left foot. Throw.
Extra-Base Hits	To left field and center field—You're the relay man. To right field—Cover 2nd base, and direct the relay.

3RD BASE

Position	Normal position is about 12 feet from the line and 6 feet deeper than the base. If the batter has a tendency to pull the ball, guard the line. If the batter bunts often, play closer.
Bunting Situation	Observe the 3rd-base coach when he gives the sign. Watch the batter's feet and hands. He may tip off the bunt. If it's a bunt, listen to the catcher for instructions. On a sacrifice bunt to you, with a runner on 1st base, make the throw to 1st base. Then return quickly to 3rd base to prevent the base runner's advancing to 3rd base. With 2 strikes on the batter, play deeper.
Surprise Bunt	Charge to the inside of the ball. Pick up the ball with the bare hand, off the right foot. In one continual motion, flip the ball underhanded, off the left foot.
Fielding	Cut off any slow ground ball hit toward the shortstop.
Double Play	Make sure the first throw is good. Don't hurry the throw. Throw the ball to 2nd base about chest high.

OUTFIELD

Playing Conditions	Know the roughness of the terrain—It may help in fielding ground balls. You can test the wind by checking the foul-line flag or by tossing grass into the air. Know how far you are from the fence (if playing in an enclosed area), and know how the ball will bounce off the fence.
Position	Adjust to the left- and right-handed batters, even more if the batter is a pull hitter.
Stance	The toes should point slightly outward. The knees should be bent slightly. The hands should be on the knees or hanging down. The weight should be distributed evenly on the balls of the feet. On each pitch, rock forward slightly on the balls of your feet.
Fielding	Use the cross-over step. If the ball is hit to your right, step first with the left foot. If the ball is hit to your left, step first wih the right foot. *Ground balls* If the play must be made in a hurry, rush in and play the ball as an infielder would. If there is no hurry, drop down on one knee. Back up other fielders—Take nothing for granted.

Fly balls

If the sun is in your eyes, use your glove to shade your eyes—It's larger than the bare hand.

Use two hands to catch the ball.

Balls above the letters should be caught with the fingers up. Balls below the letters should be caught with the fingers down.

The hands should give slightly when you catch the ball.

On a tag-up situation, catch the ball on your throwing-hand side.

Talk to each other about who is to catch the ball.

    Call: I've got it.

    Answer: Take it—Take it.

Give directions to each other about how close one is to the fence or a hazard.

Give directions about where to throw the ball.

Fly balls hit directly over your head (Shallow)

Don't backpedal. Turn and run back, keeping your eyes on the ball from over your shoulder.

Fly balls hit directly over your head (Deep)

Turn and run to where you think the ball will land.

If there is a strong wind, make both turns (away from the ball and back toward the ball) in the direction the wind is blowing.

Throwing

Taking too many steps is wrong. The runner is advancing with each extra step you take.

Throw the ball overhanded. The spin should be backward, or the ball will bounce slightly to the side when it hits the ground.

Throw the ball low, so it can be cut off.

Short distance—No bounce.

Long distance—One bounce.

DEFENSIVE SITUATIONS

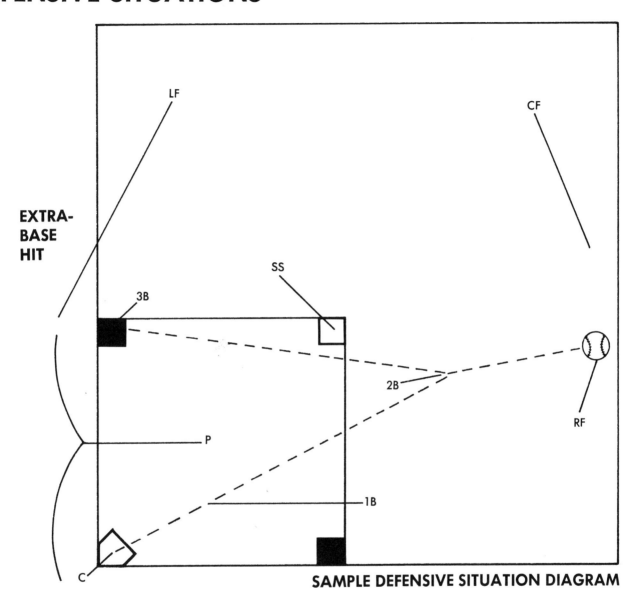

EXTRA-BASE HIT

LF

CF

SS

3B

2B

RF

P

1B

C

SAMPLE DEFENSIVE SITUATION DIAGRAM

Key to the defensive situation diagrams

■   Base runners

Ⓞ   Where ball is hit

――――   Solid lines: where each player goes

------   Broken lines: where ball is thrown

In many of the following defensive situations, where you throw the ball may be influenced by the following: score, number of outs, inning, depth of ball, number of base runners, speed of base runners, and strength of arm.

BASES EMPTY

Bunt

Left

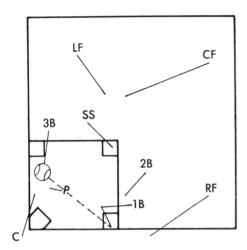

Center

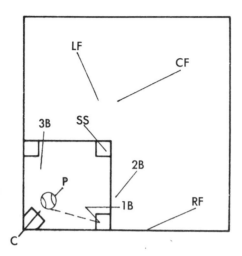

Right

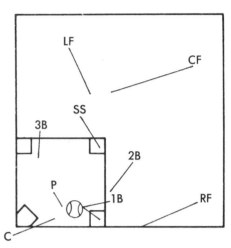

Single

Left

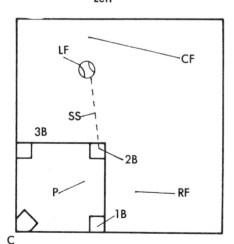

Center

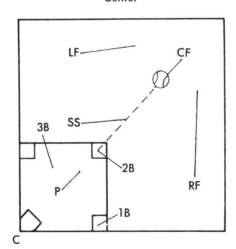

Right

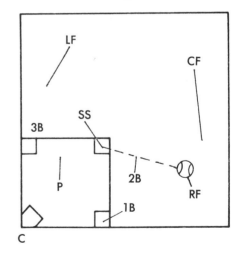

26

Extra-Base Hit

Left	Center	Right
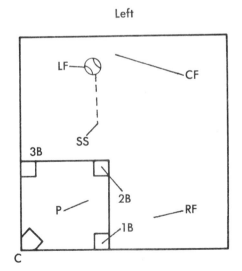	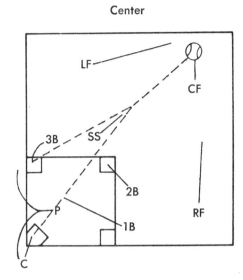	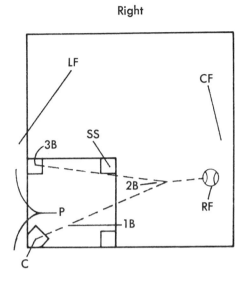

Outfield Fly

Left	Center	Right
	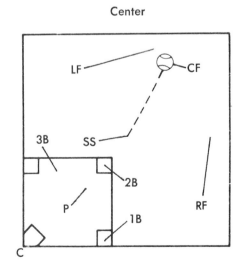	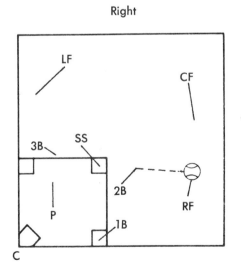

Sacrifice Bunt

Left	Center	Right
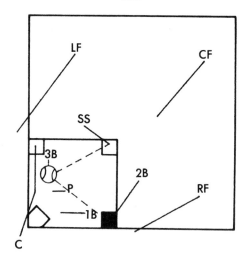	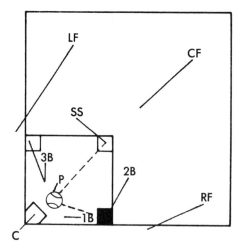	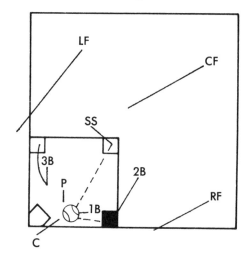

Single

Left	Center	Right
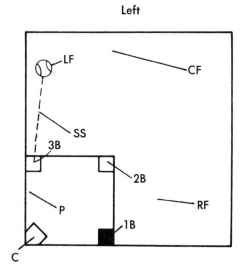	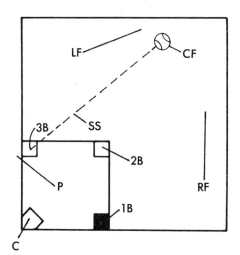	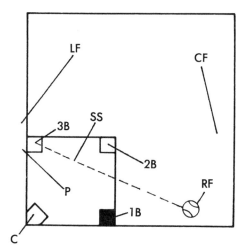

Extra-Base Hit

Left	Center	Right
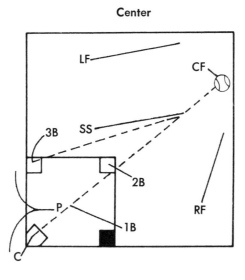		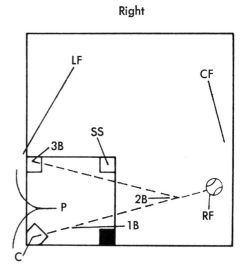

Outfield Fly

Left	Center	Right

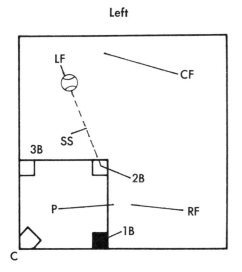

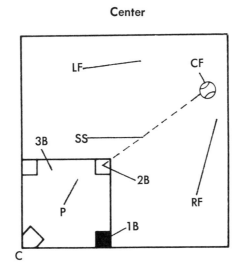

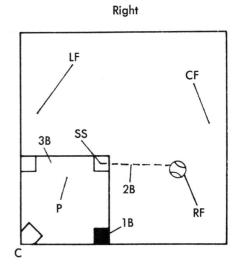

Sacrifice Bunt

Left
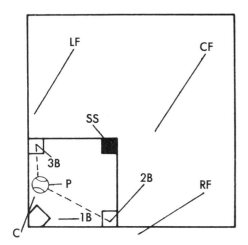

Center
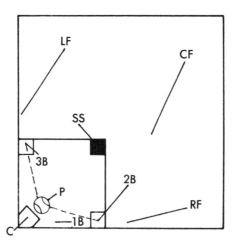

Right
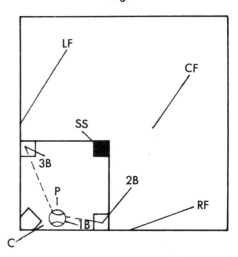

Single

Left
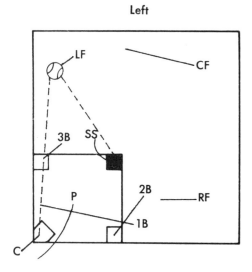

Center
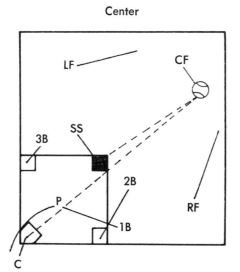

Right
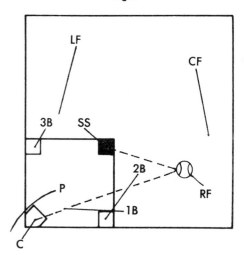

Extra-Base Hit

Left
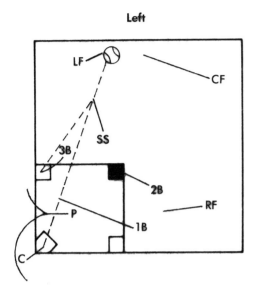

Center
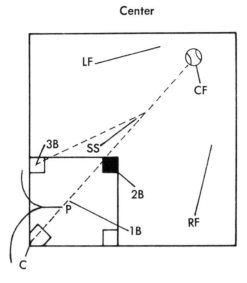

Right
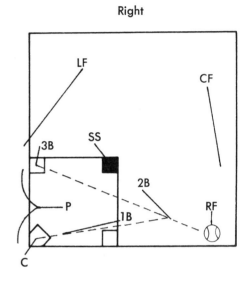

Outfield Fly

Left
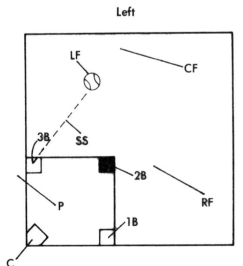

Center
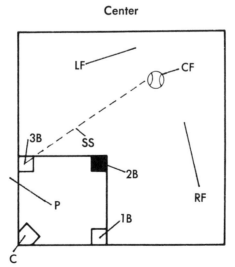

Right
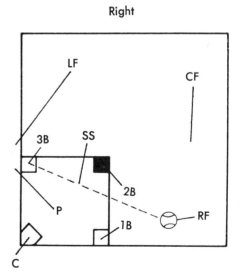

Squeeze Bunt

Left	Center	Right
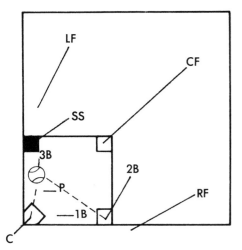	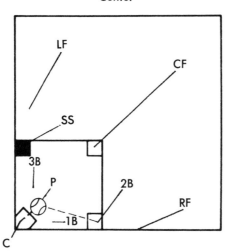	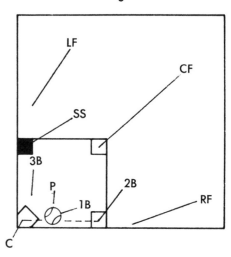

Single

Left	Center	Right
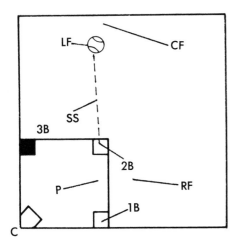	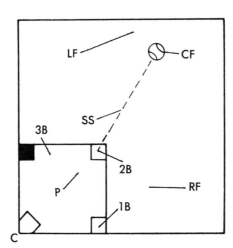	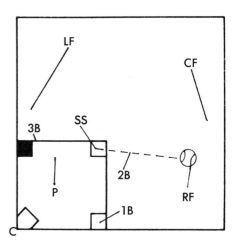

Extra-Base Hit

Left	Center	Right
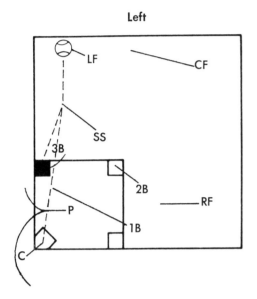	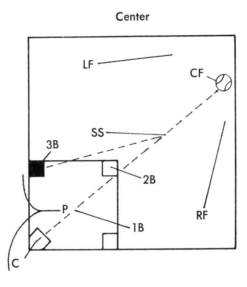	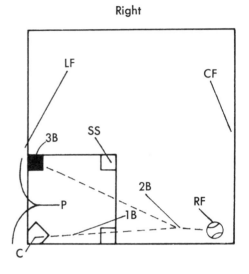

Outfield Fly

Left	Center	Right
	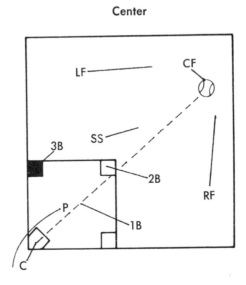	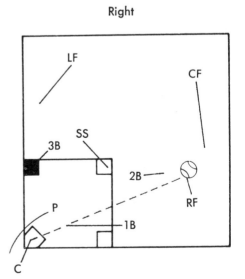

Sacrifice Bunt

Left	Center	Right
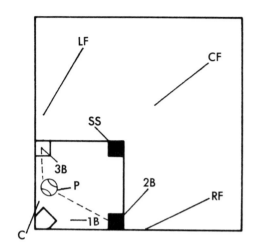	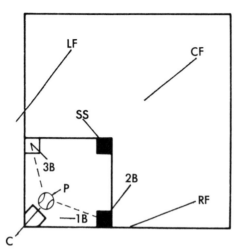	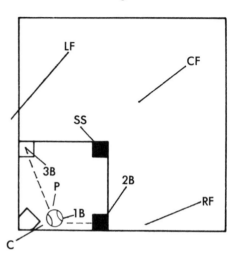

Single

Left	Center	Right
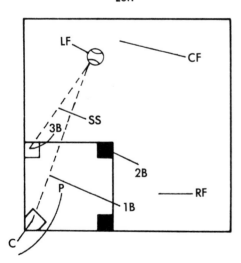	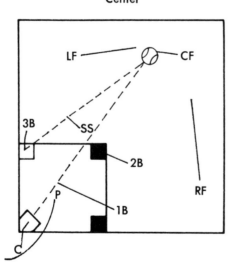	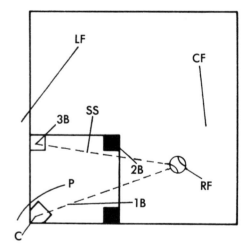

Extra-Base Hit

Left	Center	Right
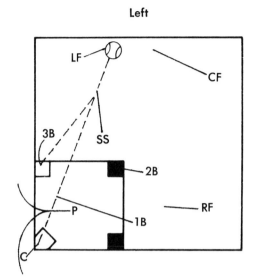	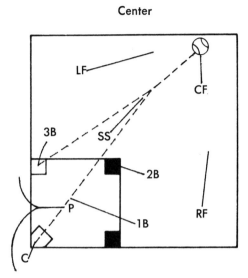	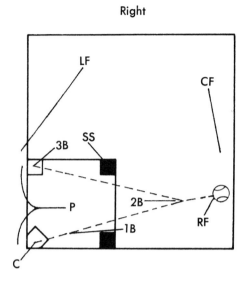

Outfield Fly

Left	Center	Right
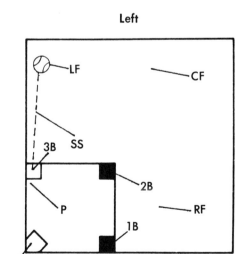	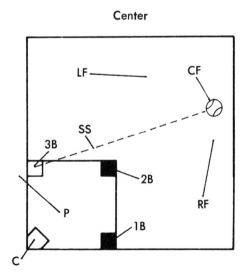	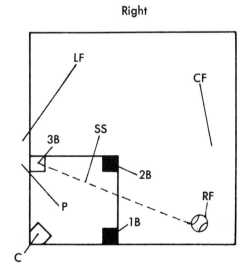

Squeeze Bunt

Left
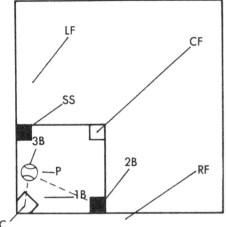

Center
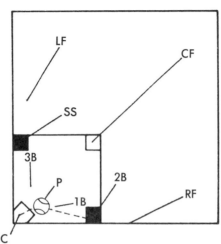

Right
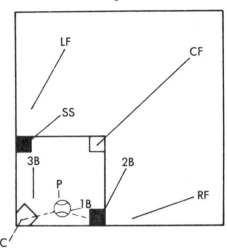

Single

Left
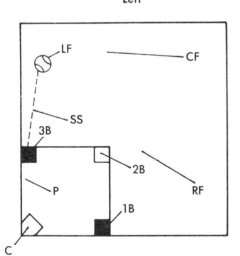

Center
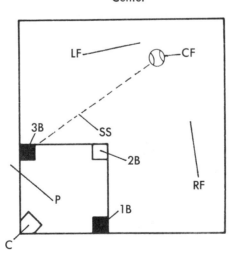

Right
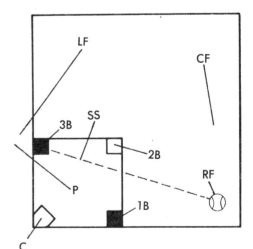

Extra-Base Hit

Left
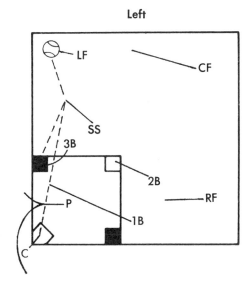

Center
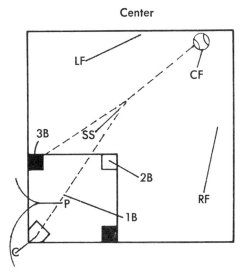

Right
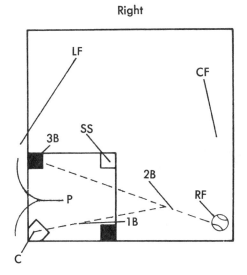

Outfield Fly

Left
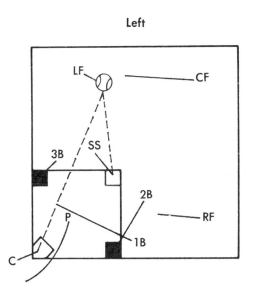

Center
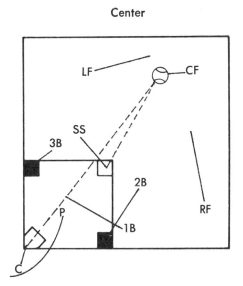

Right
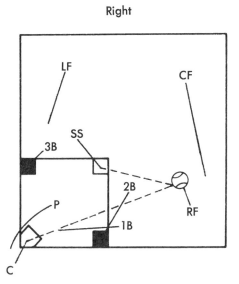

RUNNERS ON 2ND AND 3RD BASE

Squeeze Bunt

Left
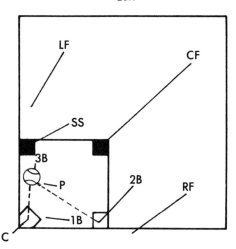

Center
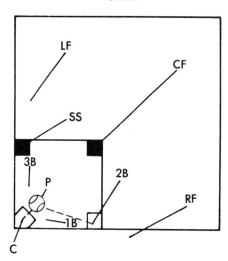

Right
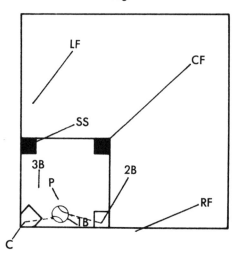

Single

Left
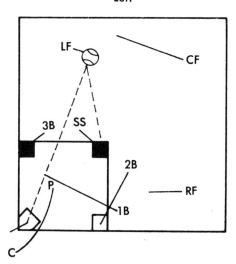

Center
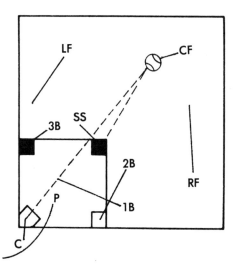

Right
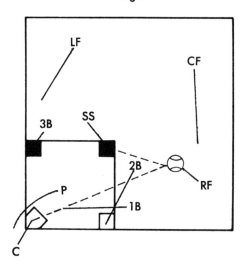

Extra-Base Hit

Left
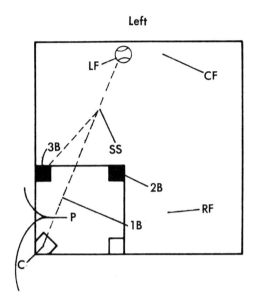

Center
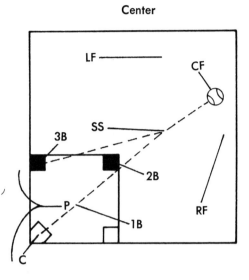

Right
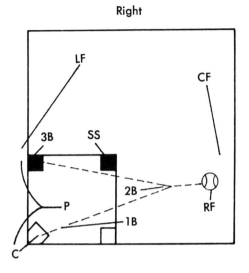

Outfield Fly

Left
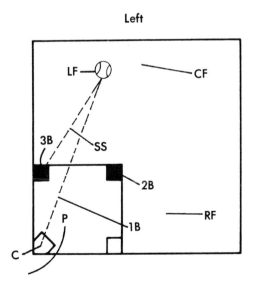

Center
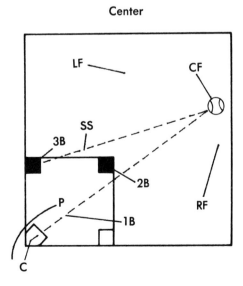

Right
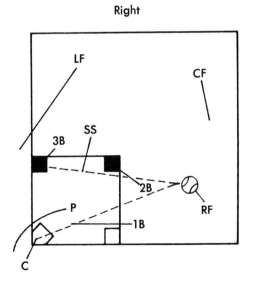

RUNNERS ON ALL BASES

Squeeze Bunt

Left	Center	Right
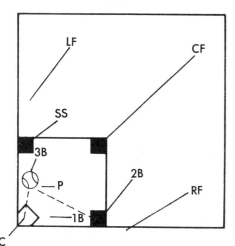	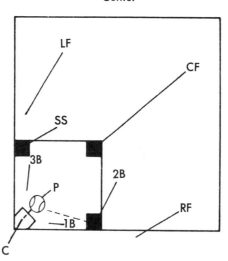	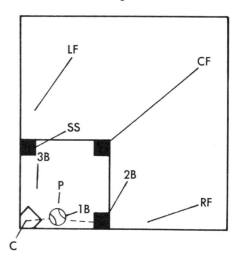

Single

Left	Center	Right
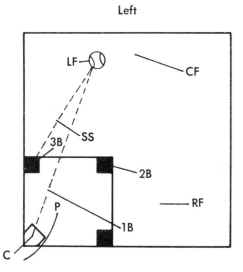	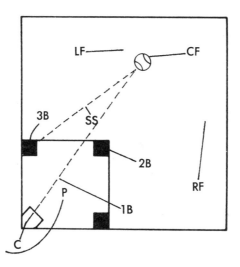	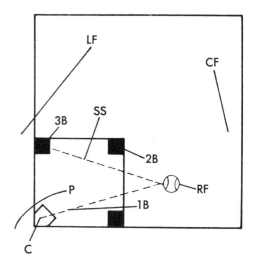

Extra-Base Hit

Left	Center	Right
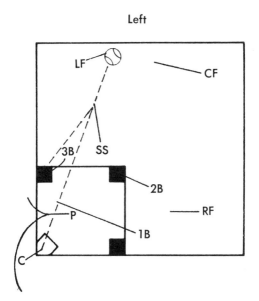	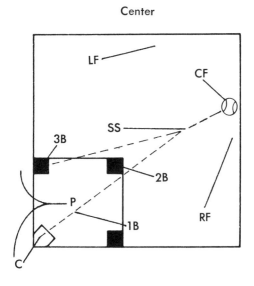	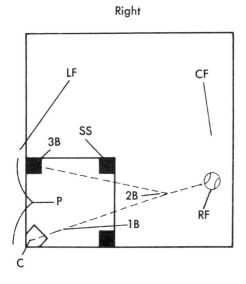

Outfield Fly

Left	Center	Right
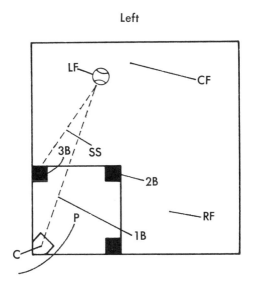	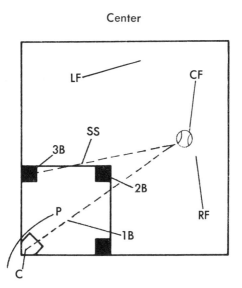	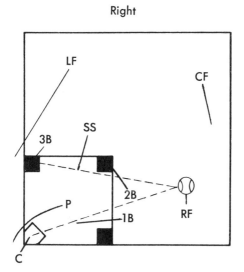

Runner on 3rd

2nd baseman or SS should back up catcher's return throw.

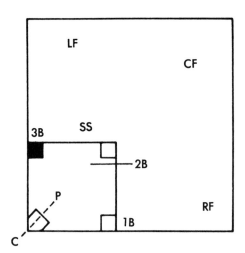

Pop Foul to Catcher

Runners—1st and 3rd

Run ball toward home, watching both runners for tag-up.

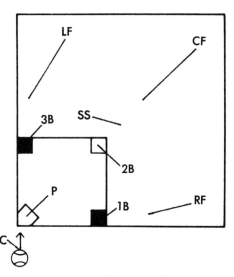

Wild Pitch

Runners—1st and 3rd

Catcher listens to pitcher for instructions either to throw or to hold the ball (see page 19).

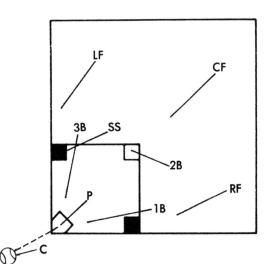

Double Steal

Runners—1st and 3rd

Catcher (a) throws to pitcher as if throwing to a bag or (b) throws to bag. The 1st baseman directs 2nd baseman to "Cut" (be ready to throw) or to "Let go" (let the ball go through).

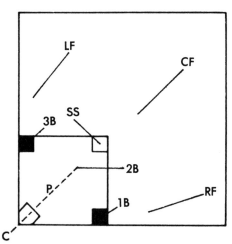

Pop Foul Behind 1st base

Runners—1st and 3rd

Throw to plate. Catcher directs pitcher to "Cut" or to "Let go."

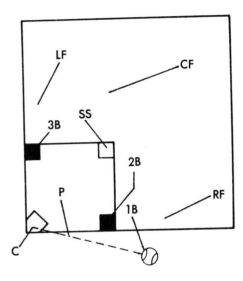

Fly-Ball Coverage

Call: I've got it.
Answer: Take it—Take it.

Player in best position calls for it.

Area is generalized.

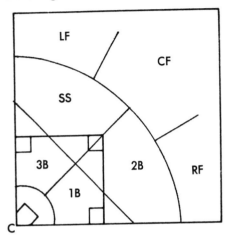

Bunt Coverage

The only bunt situation in which the **SS** covers 3rd base is when there is a runner on 3rd base.

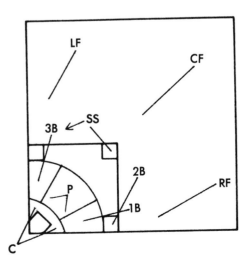

Cutoff Signals

(a) "Let it go"
   Let ball go through
(b) "Cut"
   Cut—Ready to throw
(c) "Relay"
   Cut—Relay to man calling

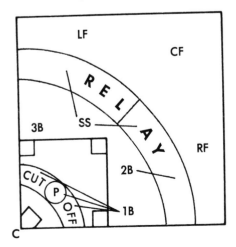

43

THROWING THE BALL AROUND THE HORN AFTER PUTOUTS

Pitcher

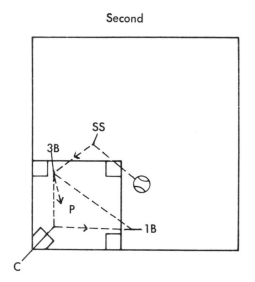

Catcher

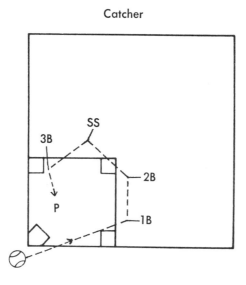

First

After infield ground ball putout

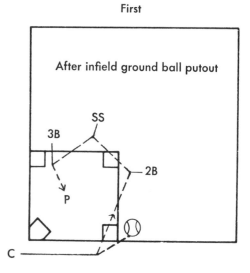

Second

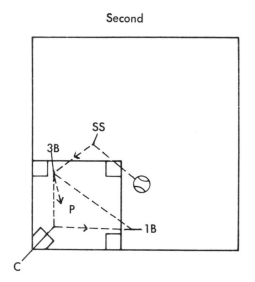

Short

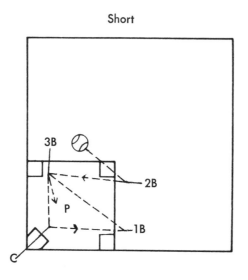

Third

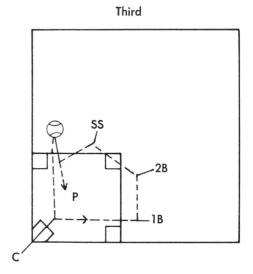

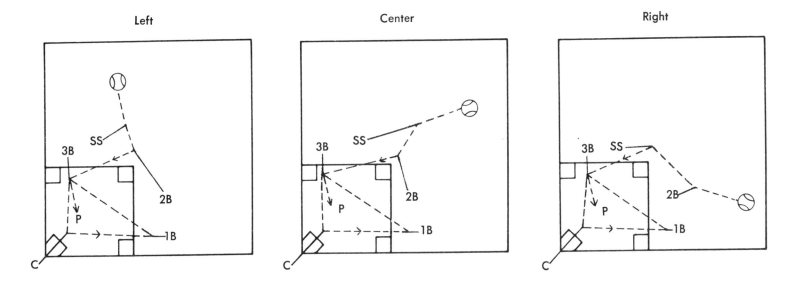

Left	Center	Right

(1) Infielders move in to shorten distance.
(2) Path of ball—Counterclockwise.
(3) Player making putout need not handle ball twice, except the 3rd baseman.
(4) Ball always returned to pitcher by the 3rd baseman.
(5) Infielder receiving outfielder's throw starts ball as if he made putout.

PREGAME WARM-UP

OUTFIELD

The coach should station himself near the pitcher's mound while hitting to the outfielders.

	Type of Ball Hit	Hit to	Thrown to
Round 1	Ground Ball	LF	2nd Base (SS Covering, 2B Backing)
	Ground Ball	CF	2nd Base (SS Covering, 2B Backing)
	Ground Ball	RF	2nd Base (2B Covering, SS Backing)
Round 2	Ground Ball	LF	3rd Base
	Ground Ball	CF	3rd Base
	Ground Ball	RF	3rd Base

SS gets in line of throw for possible cutoff.

	Type of Ball Hit	Hit to	Thrown to
Round 3	Fly Ball	LF	Home Plate
	Fly Ball	CF	Home Plate
	Fly Ball	RF	Home Plate

1st baseman gets in line of throw for possible cutoff.

Another coach should continue to hit fly balls to the outfielders while the infielders are taking their warm-up (see page 56).

INFIELD

The ball is thrown around the horn (C to 1B to 2B to SS to 3B to C)

	Type of Ball Hit	Hit to	Thrown to
Round 1	Ground Ball	3B	C to 3B to C
	Ground Ball	SS	C to 2B (SS Covering) to C
	Ground Ball	2B	C to 2B (2B Covering) to C
	Ground Ball	1B	C to 1B to C
Round 2	Ground Ball	3B	1B to C
(Getting 1	Ground Ball	SS	1B to C
out)	Ground Ball	2B	1B to C
	Ground Ball	1B	3B to C
Round 3	Ground Ball	3B	1B to C
(Getting 1	Ground Ball	SS	1B to C
out)	Ground Ball	2B	1B to C
	Ground Ball	1B	3B to C

Round 4	Ground Ball	3B	2B (2B Covering) to 1B to C
(Getting 2	Ground Ball	SS	2B (2B Covering) to 1B to C
out)	Ground Ball	2B	2B (SS Covering) to 1B to C
	Ground Ball	1B	2B (SS Covering) to 1B to C
Round 5	Ground Ball	3B	1B to C (Roll ball to 3B) to C
	Ground Ball	SS	1B to C (Roll ball to SS) to C
	Ground Ball	2B	1B to C (Roll ball to 2B) to C
	Ground Ball	1B	3B to C (Roll ball to 1B) to C

Round 6 Infielder charges ball rolled by catcher and flips ball underhanded to catcher and continues on to the bench (see pages 54 and 23).

Coach . . . take no more than 15 minutes for your team's turn on the field.

PRACTICE TECHNIQUES

DRILLS

CIRCLING THE BASES

Purpose:
To practice the proper arc in rounding the bases
To practice touching inside corner of base with left foot
To check runner's speed (use stopwatch)
(See page 13)

_____ _____ Path of runner
X   X   X   Players waiting their turn

THROWING THE BALL AROUND THE HORN

Purpose:
To practice quick release of the ball

To put fun into practice by making a contest out of the drill (each team tries to beat the others)

Procedure:
Divide the squad into four or five equally talented teams of five.

Time each team in throwing the ball around the horn (use stopwatch).

After throwing it around (C to 1B to 2B to SS to 3B to C), try it the opposite way (C to 3B, etc).

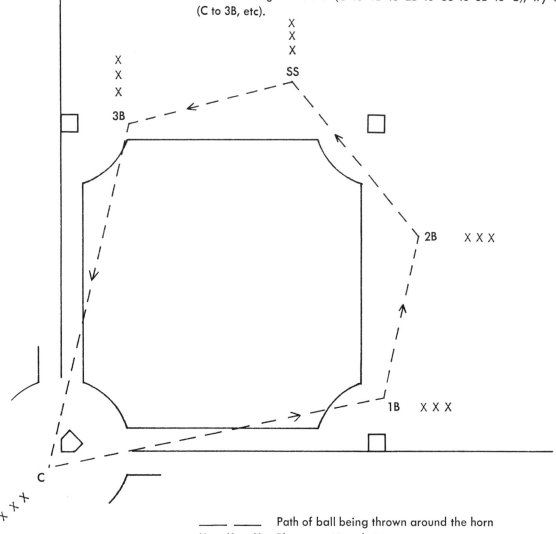

```
_____  _____   Path of ball being thrown around the horn
  X    X    X   Players waiting their turn
```

52

Purpose:

To make the pitcher automatically break toward 1st base on ground ball to the right

To teach the pitcher the proper angle toward 1st base

Procedure:

Pitcher breaks to a point 20 to 25 feet from 1st base.

He curves just inside the baseline, takes the throw, and touches 1st base with the right foot.

(See pages 18 and 21)

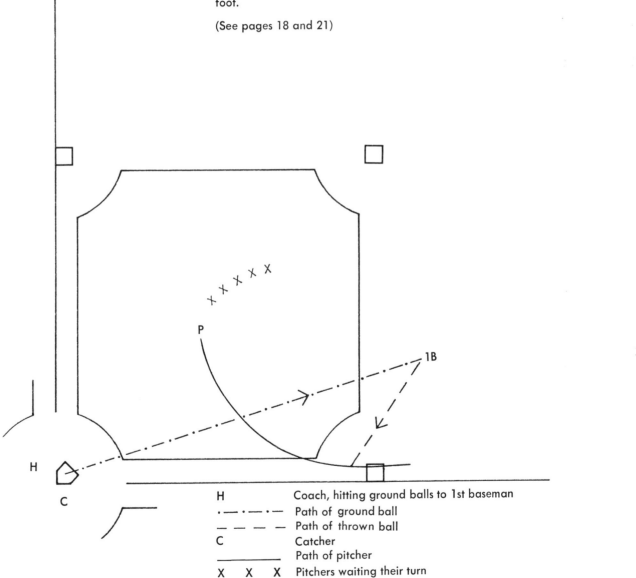

H	Coach, hitting ground balls to 1st baseman
· — · — · —	Path of ground ball
— — — —	Path of thrown ball
C	Catcher
_____	Path of pitcher
X X X	Pitchers waiting their turn

Purpose:
To practice barehanded pick-up-and-throw

Procedure:
Lay 3 balls side by side about 3 feet apart well up on the infield grass.
The 3rd baseman charges the inside ball (as in illustration).
He picks up the ball with the bare hand, off the right foot, and
in one continual motion he flips the ball underhanded, off the left foot.
Each of the three players in line fields a ball.
The balls are returned for another round.

(See page 23)

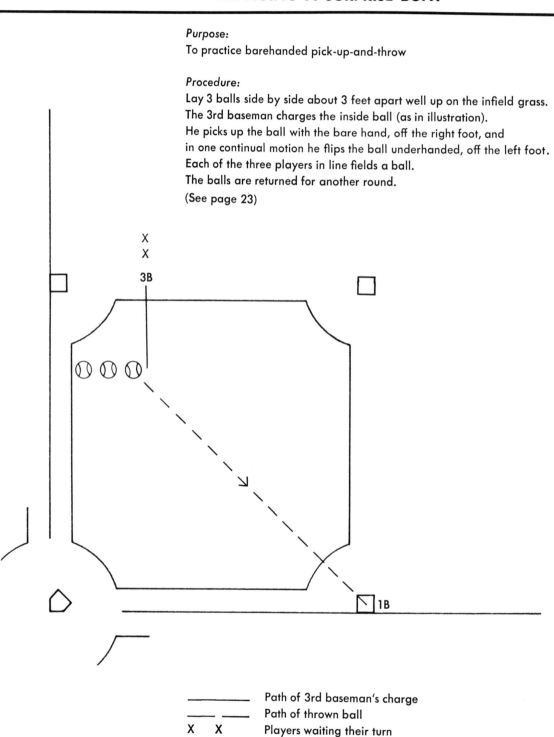

———————	Path of 3rd baseman's charge
—— —— ——	Path of thrown ball
X X	Players waiting their turn

4-WAY INFIELD PRACTICE

Purpose:
To give each infielder 4 times as many ground balls as he would field in ordinary infield practice

Procedure:
Each coach hits ground balls to the infielder directly opposite him.
If there is more than one player in a position, players rotate.

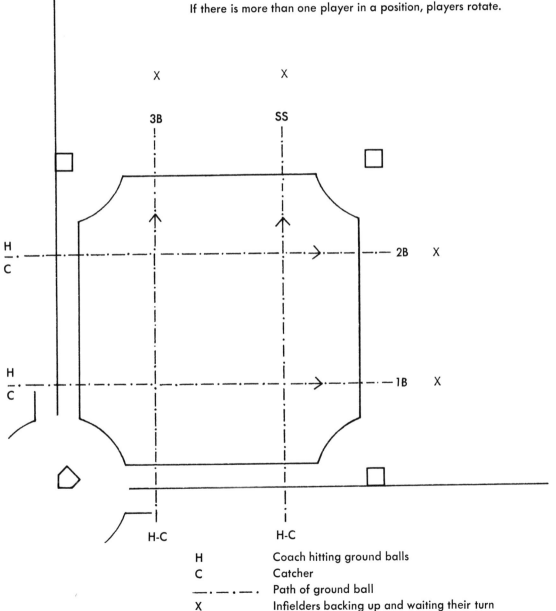

H	Coach hitting ground balls
C	Catcher
—.—.—.	Path of ground ball
X	Infielders backing up and waiting their turn

OUTFIELD "GROUND BALL—FLY BALL" PRACTICE

Purpose:
To practice fielding ground balls and fly balls to the left and right

Procedure:
Hit each outfielder a ground ball to his right.
Hit each outfielder a ground ball to his left.
Hit each outfielder a fly ball to his right.
Hit each outfielder a fly ball to his left.

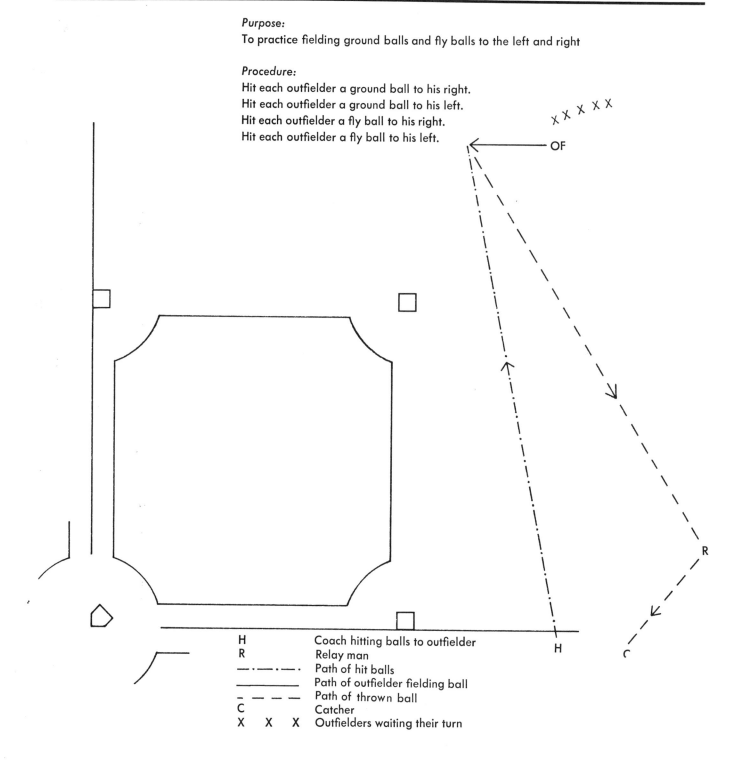

H	Coach hitting balls to outfielder
R	Relay man
—.—.—.	Path of hit balls
——————	Path of outfielder fielding ball
— — — —	Path of thrown ball
C	Catcher
X X X	Outfielders waiting their turn

CONSTRUCTION OF PRACTICE EQUIPMENT

BATTING TEE

Purpose:
To practice a level swing on high, medium, and low pitches
To practice swinging at inside and outside pitches

Automobile lower radiator hose (standard size)
   Length 10½"
   Inside diameter 1½"

"Full round" wooden rod
   Height—Depends on height of batter
   Diameter 1⅝"

   3 wooden rods to be cut—One each for high, medium, and low pitches
   Radiator hose is interchangeable

2⅝"

10½"

2"

Ground level

12"

Wooden rod is to be pounded 12" into the ground.

If in the process the end being pounded on becomes damaged, turn the rod over and slip the radiator hose on the smooth end.

STRING-BALL

Purpose:
For young batters to practice their swing without the fear of being hit

Procedure:
A player whirls the ball above his head.
Batter swings from about 12 feet away.

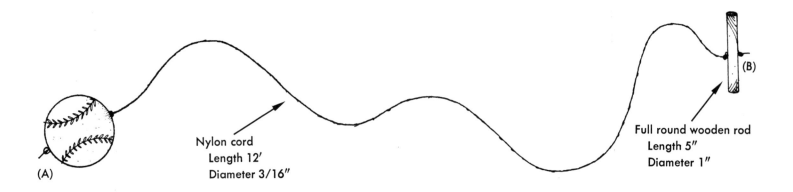

(A)

Nylon cord
Length 12'
Diameter 3/16"

Full round wooden rod
Length 5"
Diameter 1"

(B)

Drill ¼" hole through baseball and wooden rod.

Burn ends of nylon cord slightly to melt fibers together.

After inserting nylon cord through baseball and handle:

Tie several knots on the outside of (A) ball and (B) handle, forming big knots at both ends.

Burn knots A and B slightly to melt fibers together. It is very important that knots A and B be large enough and stay melted together so as not to come untied and let the ball or handle slip off.

Tie a small knot inside of the ball and handle to keep them from slipping up on string.

Possible contest: See who can hit the ball the most times out of 10 swings.

PITCHING STRINGS

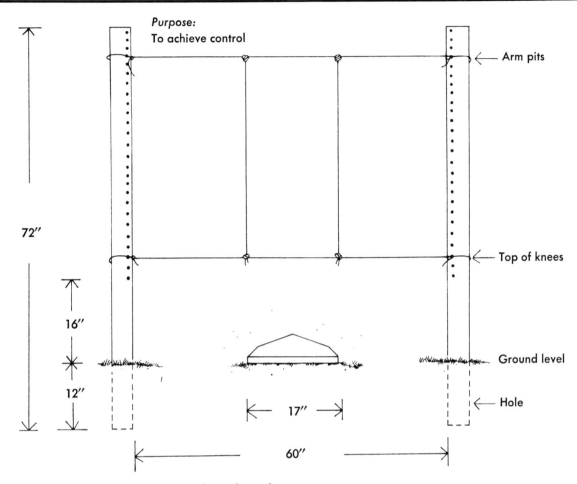

Purpose:
To achieve control

72″

16″

12″

17″

60″

← Arm pits

← Top of knees

Ground level

← Hole

Full round wooden rods
   Diameter 1⅝″
   ¼″ holes are drilled every 2″ from top down to 28″ from the bottom
Horizontal nylon cords
   Length 72″
   Diameter 3/16″
   Burn the ends of the nylon cord slightly to melt fibers together.
   Adjust the cords to the "strike zone" of the batters in your age group.
Vertical nylon cords
   Length 48″
   Diameter 3/16″
   Burn the ends of the nylon cord slightly to melt fibers together.
   Tie 17″ apart to horizontal cords. A small piece of tape should be applied to hold
   the 4 tied areas in place.

SLIDING PIT

Purpose:
To practice feetfirst, hook, and bent-leg slides
(These slides are explained on pages 13 and 14)

Construction:
Dig a hole 12′ x 12′ x 1′.
Fill the hole with 5⅓ cubic yards of sand.

Equipment:
1 base
2 base posts, 2 base straps (to tie down base)
Rake

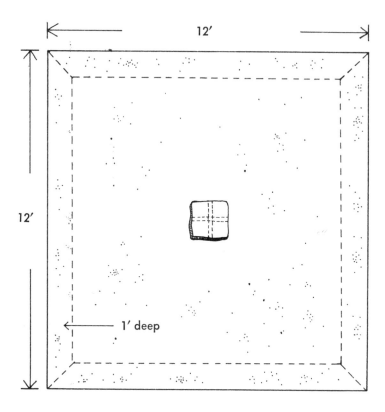

12′

12′

1′ deep

Possible contest: Have each player perform a certain slide, and choose the one who per-
forms best. Repeat with a different type of slide.

PLAYING FIELD

CONSTRUCTION OF FIELD FACILITIES

BACKSTOP

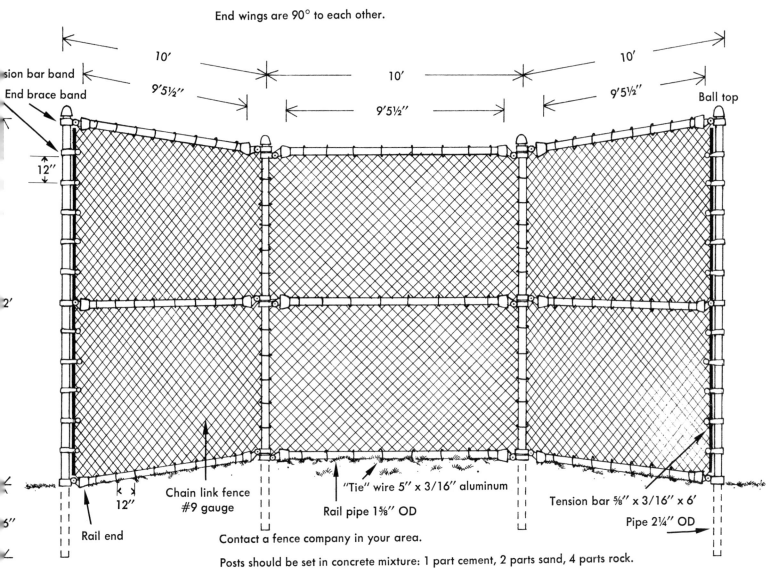

End wings are 90° to each other.

10'   10'   10'

9'5½"   9'5½"   9'5½"

sion bar band

End brace band

Ball top

12'

12"   2'

6"

Rail end

12"

Chain link fence #9 gauge

"Tie" wire 5" x 3/16" aluminum

Rail pipe 1⅝" OD

Tension bar ⅝" x 3/16" x 6'

Pipe 2¼" OD

Contact a fence company in your area.

Posts should be set in concrete mixture: 1 part cement, 2 parts sand, 4 parts rock.

Although rail pipe is 9'5½", it should be cut on the job after vertical posts are set to get exact measurement.

Chain link fence (#9 gauge, length 30', height 12'). Knuckle end is preferred over barbed end.

The bottom rail is on the ground surface, but it should be covered with loose dirt.

63

Seating Capacity, 12 to 15

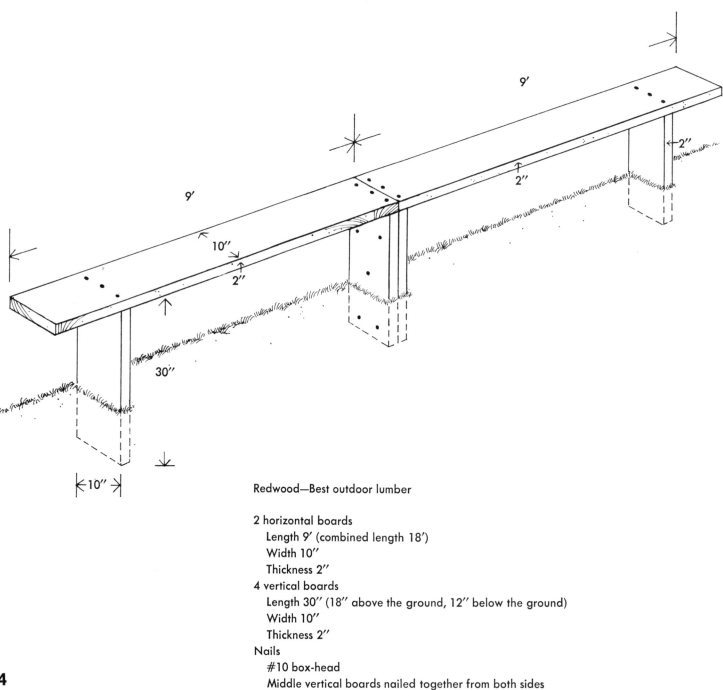

Redwood—Best outdoor lumber

2 horizontal boards
  Length 9' (combined length 18')
  Width 10"
  Thickness 2"
4 vertical boards
  Length 30" (18" above the ground, 12" below the ground)
  Width 10"
  Thickness 2"
Nails
  #10 box-head
  Middle vertical boards nailed together from both sides

BAT RACK

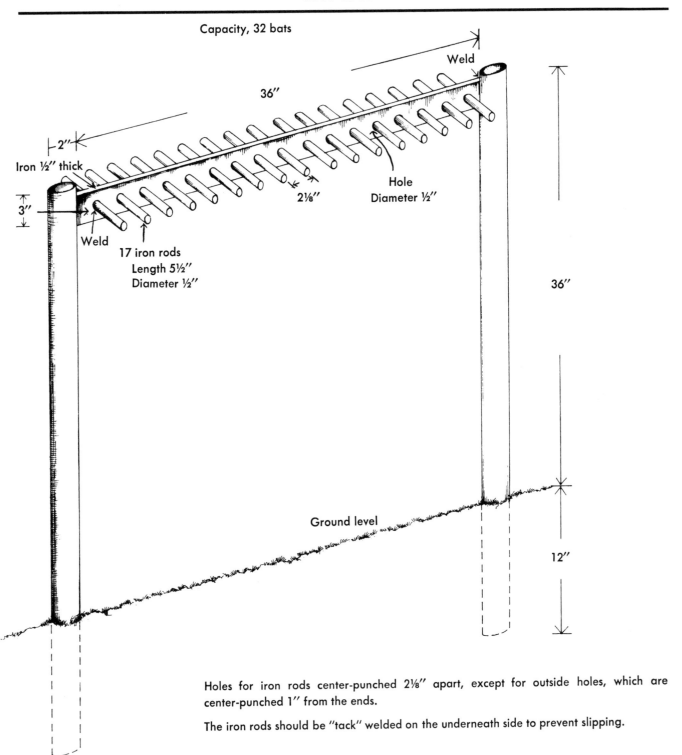

Capacity, 32 bats

Weld

36"

2"

Iron ½" thick

3"

Weld

Hole
Diameter ½"

2⅛"

17 iron rods
Length 5½"
Diameter ½"

36"

Ground level

12"

Holes for iron rods center-punched 2⅛" apart, except for outside holes, which are center-punched 1" from the ends.

The iron rods should be "tack" welded on the underneath side to prevent slipping.

65

Purpose:
To protect the pitcher from low-hit balls during batting practice

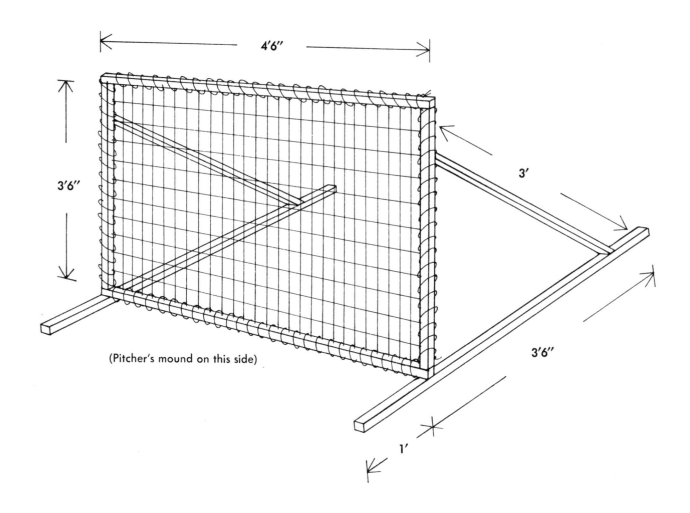

(Pitcher's mound on this side)

Frame is made of 1″ square hollow metal tubing. All connections are welded.

Protective screen (2″ x 4″ welded wire fence) is connected to frame with baling wire. Baling wire is spiraled around frame and outer edge of screen. Separate section of wire is used for each of the four sides.

1ST BASEMAN'S SCREEN

Purpose:
To protect the 1st baseman from being hit by ball during batting practice, when infield practice is going on simultaneously

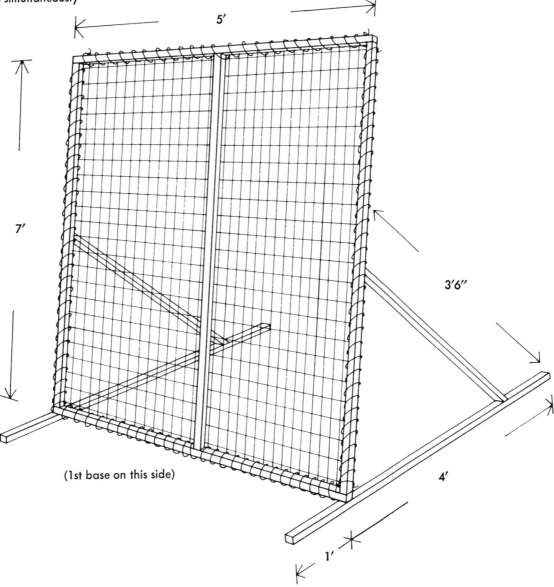

5'

7'

3'6"

(1st base on this side)

4'

1'

Frame is made of 1" square hollow metal tubing. All frame connections are welded.

Protective screen (2" x 4" welded wire fence) is connected to frame with baling wire. Baling wire is spiraled around frame and outer edge of screen. Separate section of wire is used for each of the four sides.

LAYOUT AND MAINTENANCE OF THE PLAYING FIELD

LAYING OUT THE DIAMOND

Objective:
To lay the diamond out in a direction that keeps the sun out of the pitcher's, batter's, and catcher's eyes by running the direction of home plate to 1st base in either of two directions, west to east or north to south

The Turf:
Should be firm but slightly spongy and should provide good footing for maximum speed.

Should provide proper elevation and slope for good drainage.

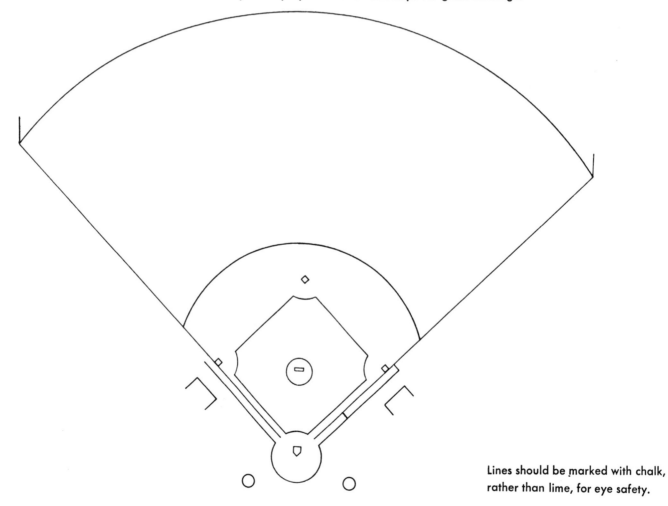

Lines should be marked with chalk, rather than lime, for eye safety.

Coach's Box:
Sand or gravel

When boards (2 x 4s) are used for outline, they should be flush with the ground to avoid tripping.

On-Deck Circle:
Sand

Grassed Area:
Bermuda grass

Sodding and seeding season depends on section of country you live in (check with local lawn service company in your area).

Aerate.

Water occasionally.

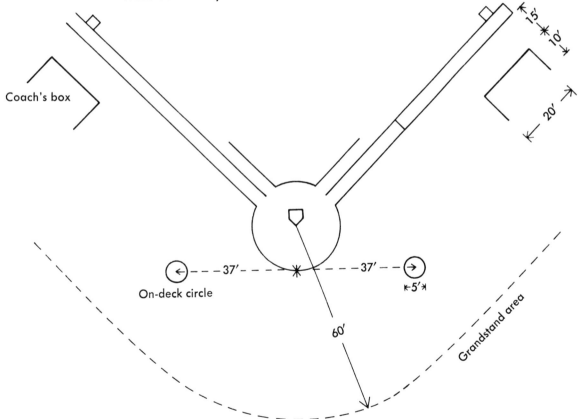

Gradual slope from home-plate circle to backstop for proper drainage

Soil:
Foundation of dark clay
Mixture of ordinary dirt and sand on the surface
Additional mixture of dirt and sand on the 3rd-base side to ensure safety for sliding

Repairs:
The area should be clay-packed, smoothed, and watered after each practice or game.

Base lines 90°

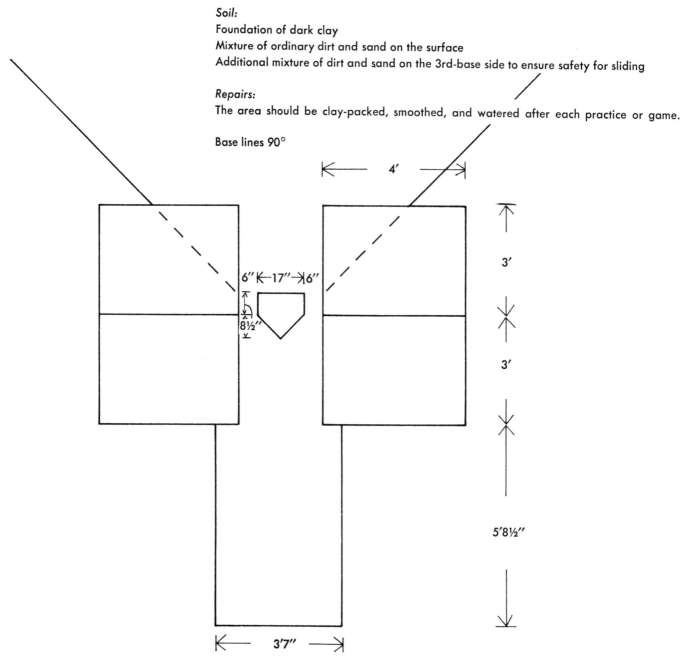

The grass line surrounding home plate and catcher's area—13' radius from back of home plate

The area should be almost level but elevated 3″ or 4″ to ensure proper drainage.

1ST AND 3RD BASE PATHS

Soil:
Brown adobe dirt with dark-colored clay and sand
Base paths should be rounded slightly for good drainage.

Repairs:
Should be raked and watered after each practice or game.

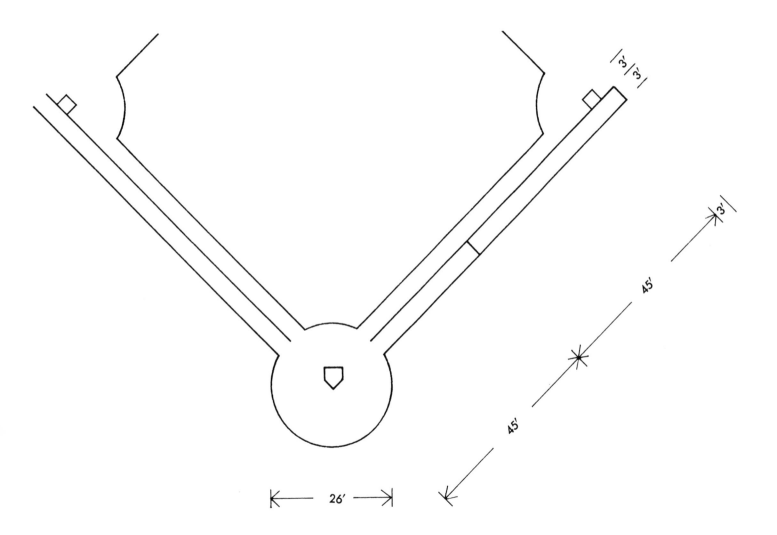

Base distance (1st base to 3rd base) 127' 3⅜'', measured from farthest edge

Grassed Area:
Bermuda grass
Sodding and seeding season depends on section of the country you live in (check with local lawn service company in your area).
Fertilize.
Aerate.
Water occasionally.
Keep grass short.

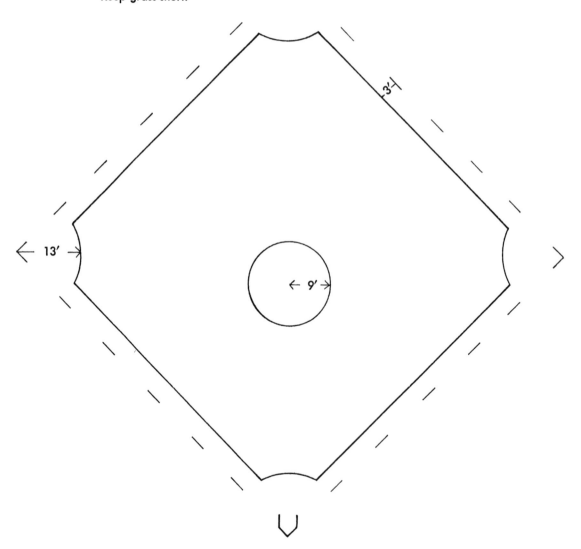

Gradual slope from edge of pitcher's circle to base paths and infield "skinned" area to ensure proper drainage

PITCHER'S MOUND

Soil:
Mixture of ordinary dirt and a large percentage of dark-colored clay
Large chunks of clay should be used in flat surface area and in area extending several feet in front of flat surface.
Thin layer of sand should cover the surface to prevent crusting.
The soil should never be screened.

Repair:
The mound should be clay-packed, smoothed, and watered after each practice or game.

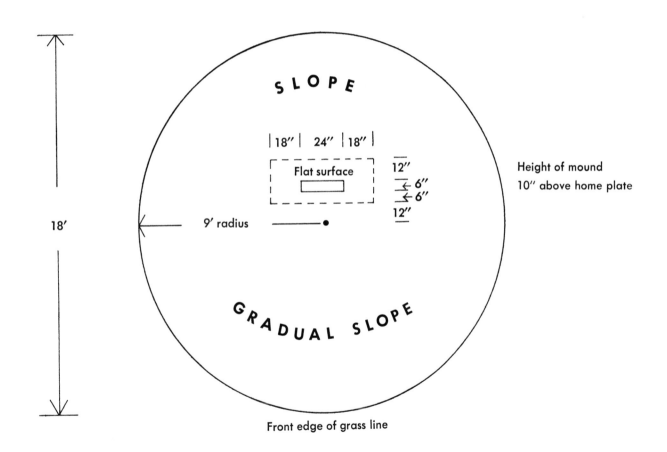

Distance from front of pitcher's rubber to back of home plate—60'6"

INFIELD "SKINNED" AREA

To level foundation:
Disk—To mix up the soil (use farm disk).
Drag—To break up the soil (use nail drag, page 76).
Roll—To pack soil (use dirt roller, page 81).
Water and let dry.

Drag.
Level—To fill in low areas (use dirt leveler, page 80).
Roll.
Water and let dry.

Drag.
Level.
Roll.
Water and let dry.

Topsoil:
Spread about 10 cubic yards of topsoil—a mixture of brown adobe dirt, clay, and sand.
This will give the leveled foundation about a ¾" cushion.

To level topsoil:
Drag with nail drag.
Level.
Water and let dry.
Drag with fence drag (see page 77).

Bases:
Topsoil should be slightly thicker around bases for sliding purposes.

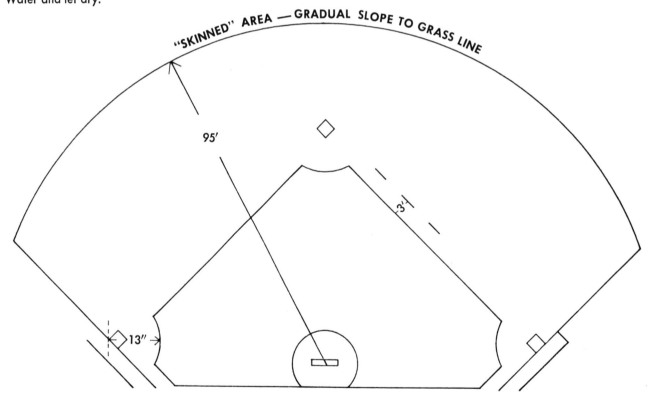

Base size—15" square
Base-path length—90' measured from back sides
Base distance—Home to 2nd base and 1st base to 3rd base—127'3⅜"

Grass:
Bermuda grass
Sodding and seeding season depends on section of country you live in (check with local lawn service company in your area).
Fertilize.
Aerate.
Water occasionally.

Foul Pole:
Foul pole is in fair territory.

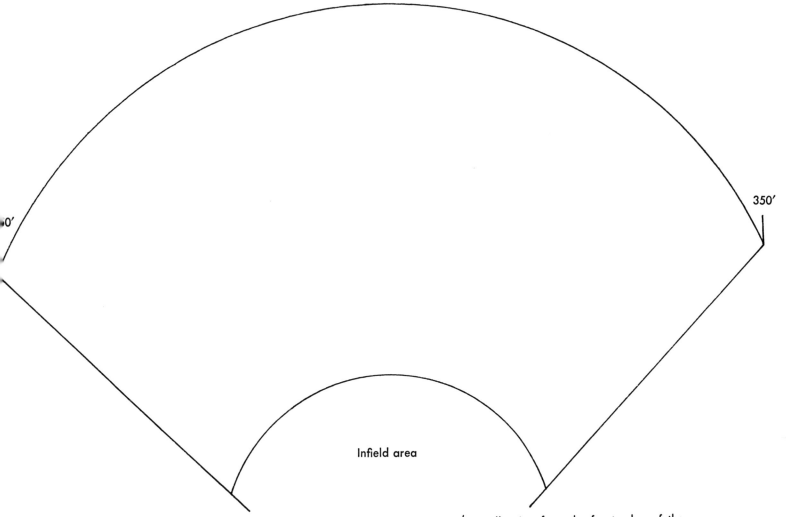

Infield area

Front edge of the outfield grass is an arc, 95′ at all points from the front edge of the pitcher's rubber.

CONSTRUCTION OF MAINTENANCE EQUIPMENT

NAIL DRAG

Purpose:
To break up soil after disking
To help level soil
To bring rocks to surface for removal

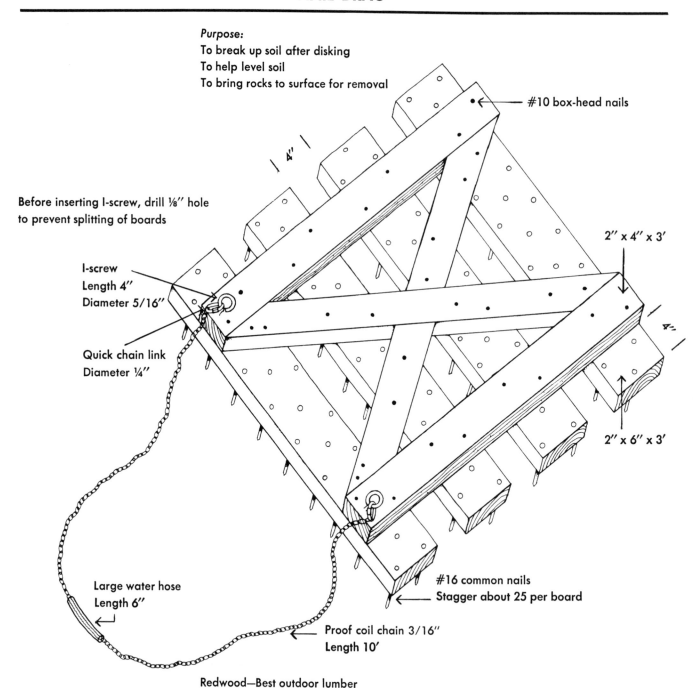

#10 box-head nails

Before inserting I-screw, drill ⅛″ hole
to prevent splitting of boards

I-screw
Length 4″
Diameter 5/16″

Quick chain link
Diameter ¼″

4″

2″ x 4″ x 3′

4″

2″ x 6″ x 3′

#16 common nails
Stagger about 25 per board

Large water hose
Length 6″

Proof coil chain 3/16″
Length 10′

Redwood—Best outdoor lumber

FENCE DRAG

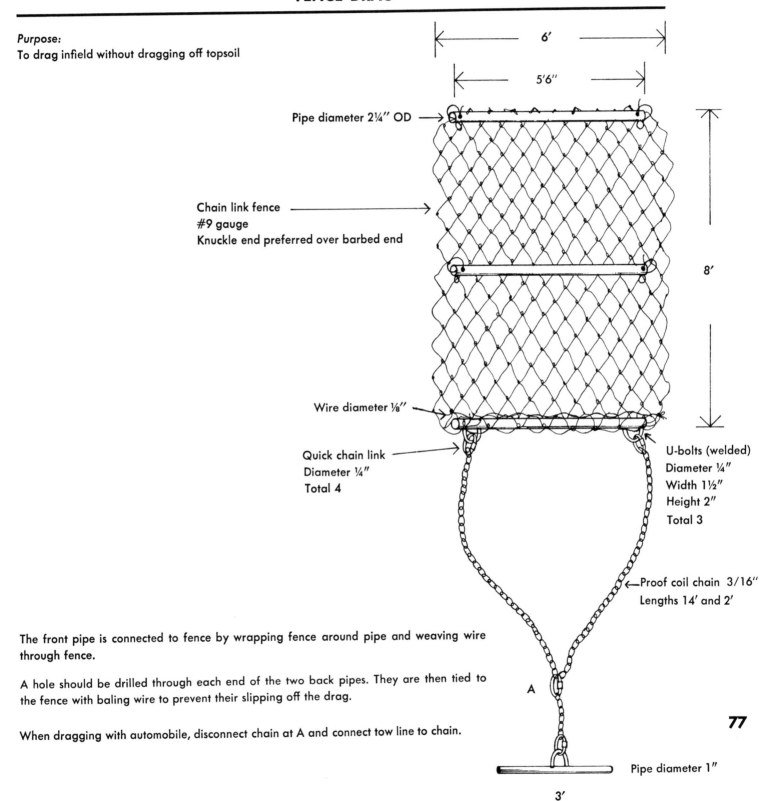

Purpose:
To drag infield without dragging off topsoil

Pipe diameter 2¼″ OD →

Chain link fence
#9 gauge
Knuckle end preferred over barbed end →

6′

5′6″

8′

Wire diameter ⅛″ →

Quick chain link
Diameter ¼″
Total 4

U-bolts (welded)
Diameter ¼″
Width 1½″
Height 2″
Total 3

←Proof coil chain 3/16″
Lengths 14′ and 2′

A

The front pipe is connected to fence by wrapping fence around pipe and weaving wire through fence.

A hole should be drilled through each end of the two back pipes. They are then tied to the fence with baling wire to prevent their slipping off the drag.

When dragging with automobile, disconnect chain at A and connect tow line to chain.

Pipe diameter 1″

3′

77

DIRT SCREEN

Purpose:
To screen small rocks from the playing field (or from new soil before it is added to the playing field)

Procedure:
Fill screen with several shovels of dirt.
With one person at each end, shake the screen; the soil will sift out, leaving only the rocks.

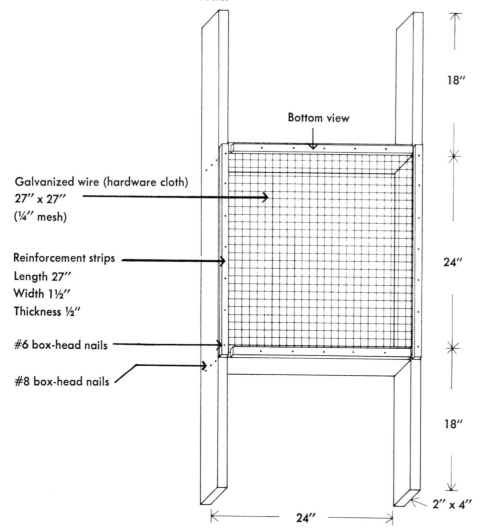

Bottom view

18″

Galvanized wire (hardware cloth) 27″ x 27″ (¼″ mesh)

Reinforcement strips
Length 27″
Width 1½″
Thickness ½″

24″

#6 box-head nails

#8 box-head nails

18″

2″ x 4″

24″

45 to 50 ⅞″ galvanized roofing nails (2″ apart) hold the screen to the 2 x 4s under the reinforcement stripping.

Redwood—Best outdoor lumber

Purpose:
To pack the dirt in the mound, batter's box, and catcher's areas

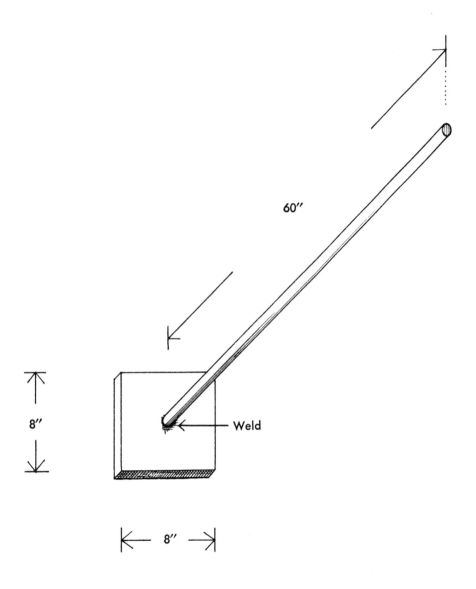

60″

8″

8″

Weld

The 8″ x 8″ section is a flat iron, thickness ½″.

The 60″ shaft is an iron rod, diameter 1″.

DIRT LEVELER

Purpose:
To level catcher's area, batter's box, pitcher's mound, and rough areas in the infield

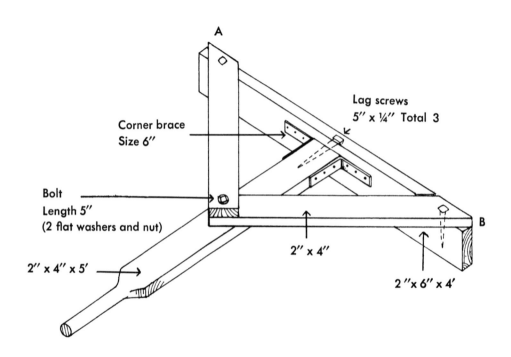

Connection A—The 2 x 4 is above the 2 x 6.

Connection B—The 2 x 4 is flush with the 2 x 6.
   (A 1½" section is cut from the 2 x 6)

Handle—Fastened 1½" from top of blade
   (Before inserting lag screws, drill ⅛" hole to prevent splitting of boards)

Redwood—Best outdoor lumber

DIRT ROLLER

Purpose:
To pack and level area around home plate and pitcher's mound

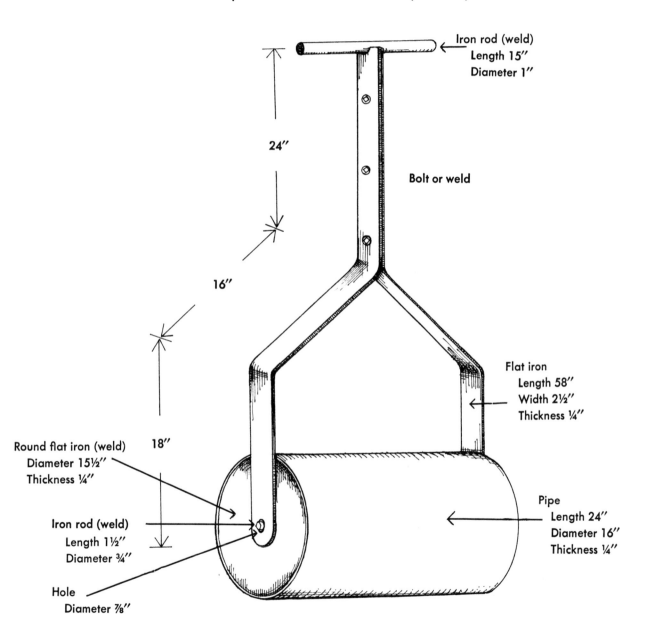

Iron rod (weld)
Length 15"
Diameter 1"

24"

Bolt or weld

16"

Flat iron
Length 58"
Width 2½"
Thickness ¼"

Round flat iron (weld)
Diameter 15½"
Thickness ¼"

18"

Pipe
Length 24"
Diameter 16"
Thickness ¼"

Iron rod (weld)
Length 1½"
Diameter ¾"

Hole
Diameter ⅞"

If bolting handle, use 1" x ¼" bolts and washers.

BATTER'S BOX OUTLINE

Purpose:
To make imprint of batter's box on ground

Procedure:
Walk on the outline.
Flip over to other side of home plate.
Walk on the outline.
Remove outline.
Chalk over the imprint.
The outside of the chalk line is even with the outside of the imprint.

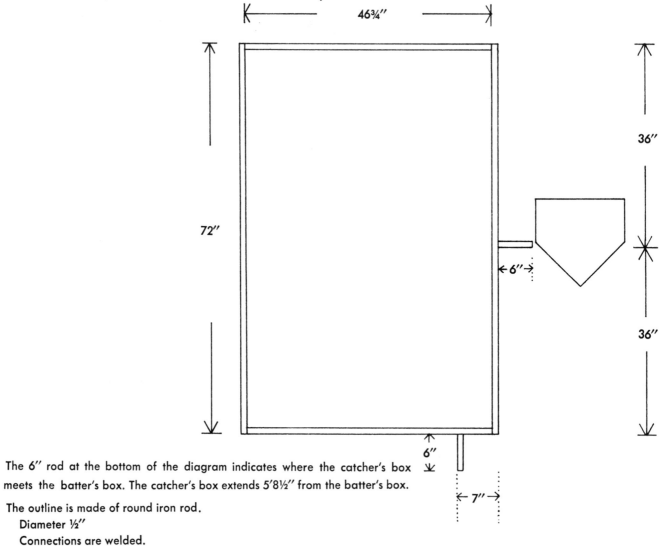

The 6" rod at the bottom of the diagram indicates where the catcher's box meets the batter's box. The catcher's box extends 5'8½" from the batter's box.

The outline is made of round iron rod.
    Diameter ½"
    Connections are welded.

APPENDICES
AND INDEX

STRUCTURE OF
ORGANIZED BASEBALL

PROFESSIONAL BASEBALL

Professional Baseball is divided into two divisions

The Major Leagues are governed by

Commissioner of Baseball ....Office: New York, New York

President of American League ....Office: New York, New York

President of National League ....Office: New York, New York

The Minor Leagues are governed by

National Association ....Offce: St. Petersburg, Florida

The National Association is not a baseball league but a board that controls minor league baseball.

The four offices above are the government of professional baseball. The combination of the two divisions make up what we call "organized baseball."

MAJOR LEAGUE TEAMS AND STADIUMS

American League

Eastern Division	Stadium	Number of Seats
Baltimore Orioles	Memorial Stadium	53,208
Boston Red Sox	Fenway Park	33,465
Cleveland Indians	Municipal Stadium	74,208
Detroit Tigers	Tiger Stadium	52,687
Milwaukee Brewers	County Stadium	53,192
New York Yankees	Yankee Stadium	57,545
Toronto Blue Jays	Exhibition Stadium	43,737
Western Division		
California Angels	Anaheim Stadium	67,335
Chicago White Sox	Comiskey Park	43,651
Kansas City Royals	Royal Stadium	40,635
Minnesota Twins	The Metrodome	55,122
Oakland Athletics	Oakland-Alameda Coliseum	50,219
Seattle Mariners	The King Dome	59,438
Texas Rangers	Arlington Stadium	41,284

National League

Eastern Division	Stadium	Number of Seats
Chicago Cubs	Wrigley Field	37,272
Montreal Expos	Olympic Stadium	58,838
New York Mets	Shea Stadium	55,300
Philadelphia Phillies	Veterans Stadium	66,507
Pittsburgh Pirates	Three Rivers Stadium	54,598
St. Louis Cardinals	Busch Memorial Stadium	50,222

Western Division		
Atlanta Braves	Atlanta Stadium	52,934
Cincinnati Reds	Riverfront Stadium	52,392
Houston Astros	Astrodome	45,000
Los Angeles Dodgers	Dodger Stadium	56,000
San Diego Padres	San Diego Stadium	51,319
San Francisco Giants	Candlestick Park	58,000

MINOR LEAGUES

AAA

International League

Charleston Charlies	Rochester Red Wings
Columbus Clippers	Syracuse Chiefs
Pawtucket Red Sox	Tidewater Tides
Richmond Braves	Toledo Mud Hens

American Association

Eastern (Division)	Western
Evansville Triplets	Denver Bears
Indianapolis Indians	Oklahoma City 89ers
Iowa Cubs	Omaha Royals
Louisville Redbirds	Wichita Aeros

Pacific Coast League

Northern (Division)	Southern
Edmonton Trappers	Albuquerque Dukes
Portland Beavers	Hawaii Islanders
Spokane Indians	Phoenix Giants
Tacoma Tigers	Salt Lake City Gulls
Vancouver Canadians	Tucson Toros

AA

Eastern League

Northern (Division)	Southern
Buffalo Bisons	Bristol Red Sox
Holyoke Millers	Reading Phillies
Lynn Sailors	Waterbury Reds
Glens Falls White Sox	West Haven A's

Southern League

Eastern (Division)	Western
Charlotte Orioles	Birmingham Barons
Columbus Astros	Chattanooga Lookouts
Jacksonville Suns	Knoxville Blue Jays
Orlando Twins	Memphis Chicks
Savannah Braves	Nashville Sounds

Texas League

Eastern (Division)	Western
Arkansas Travelers	Amarillo Gold Sox
Jackson Mets	El Paso Diablos
Shreveport Captains	Midland Cubs
Tulsa Drillers	San Antonio Dodgers

A

California League

Northern (Division)	Southern
Lodi Dodgers	Bakersfield Mariners
Modesto A's	Fresno Giants
Redwood Pioneers	Salinas Spurs
Reno Padres	San Jose Expos
Stockton Ports	Visalis Oaks

Carolina League

Northern (Division)	Southern
Alexandria Dukes	Durham Bulls
Hagerstown Suns	Kinston Blue Jays
Lynchburg Mets	Peninsula Pilots
Salem Redbirds	Winston-Salem Red Sox

Florida State League

Northern (Division)	Southern
Daytona Beach Astros	Fort Lauderdale Yankees
Lakeland Tigers	Fort Myers Royals
St. Petersburg Cardinals	Miami Marlins
Tampa Tarpons	Vero Beach Dodgers
Winter Haven Red Sox	West Palm Beach Expos

Midwest League

Northern (Division)	Southern
Appleton Foxes	Burlington Rapids Reds
Beloit Brewers	Cedar Rapids Reds
Madison Muskies	Clinton Giants
Waterloo Indians	Danville Suns
Wausau Timbers	Quad City Cubs
Wisconsin Rapids Twins	Springfield Cardinals

New York-Pennsylvania League

Yawkey (Division)	Wrigley
Auburn Astros	Batavia Trojans
Elmira Suns	Erie Cardinals
Little Falls Mets	Geneva Cubs
Oneonta Yankees	Jamestown Expos
Utica Blue Sox	Niagara Falls White Sox

South Atlantic League

Northern (Division)	Southern
Asheville Tourists	Anderson Braves
Gastonia Cardinals	Charleston Royals
Greensboro Hornets	Florence Blue Jays
Shelby Mets	Greenwood Pirates
Spartanburg Traders	Macon Peaches

Northwest League

Northern (Division)	Southern
Bellingham Mariners	Eugene Emeralds
Bend Phillies	Medford A's
Walla Walla Padres	Salem Angels

ROOKIE LEAGUES

Appalachian League

Bluefield Orioles
Bristol Tigers
Elizabeth Twins
Johnson City Cardinals
Kingsport Mets
Paintsville Yankees
Pikeville Brewers
Pulaski Braves

Gulf Coast League

Bradenton Blue Jays
Bradenton Braves
Bradenton Pirates
Bradenton Yankees
Sarasota Astros
Sarasota Cubs
Sarasota Padres
Sarasota Rangers
Sarasota Royals
Sarasota White Sox

Pioneer League

Northern   (Division)
Calgary Expos
Great Falls Giants
Lethbridge Dodgers
Medicine Hat Blue Jays

Southern
Billings Mustangs
Butte Copper Kings
Helena Phillies
Idaho Falls Athletics

PLAYING RULES AND OTHER INFORMATION

Rules and other information for various baseball organizations can be obtained by writing to the following places. (Some of the organizations' rules are free; others' will vary in price.)

Activity	Age	Address
American Legion	18 and under	American Legion Box 1055 Indianapolis, Indiana 46206
Amateur		American Amateur Baseball Congress Box 5332 Akron, Ohio 44313
Amateur		National Baseball Congress Box 1420 Wichita, Kansas 62201
Babe Ruth	13–15 16–18	Babe Ruth Baseball 524½ Hamilton Avenue Trenton, New Jersey 08609
Bronco	12 and under	Boys Baseball, Inc. Box 225 Washington, Pennsylvania 15301
Colt	15–16	Boys Baseball, Inc. Box 225 Washington, Pennsylvania 15301
Connie Mack	18 and under	American Amateur Baseball Congress Box 5332 Akron, Ohio 44313
High School	Grades 9–12	Contact your state high school athletic or activity association.
Khoury		
Atom Division	7–9	George Khoury Baseball
Bantam Division	10 and under	3222 Park Avenue
Midget Division	12 and under	St. Louis, Missouri 63104
Juvenile Division	14 and under	
Junior Division	16 and under	
Intermediate Division	18 and under	
Prep Division	20 and under	
Senior Division	No age limit	

The age cutoff date in most organizations throughout the United States is August 1. Example: If the league age is 15 to 16, and you reach your 17th birthday before August 1st, you are not eligible.

Activity	Age	Address
Little League		
Little Division	9–12	Little League Baseball, Inc.
Senior Division	13–15	Box 1127
Big Division	16–18	Williamsport, Pennsylvania 17701
Mickey Mantle	16 and under	American Amateur Baseball Congress Box 5332 Akron, Ohio 44313
Mustang	9–10	Boys Baseball, Inc. Box 225 Washington, Pennsylvania 15301
National Hot Stove	9–19	National Hot Stove Baseball League, Inc. 20 E. Main St. Alliance, Ohio 44601
N.C.A.A.	College	P.O. Box 1906 Shawnee Mission Kansas 66222
Pee Wee Reese	12 and under	American Amateur Baseball Congress Box 5332 Akron, Ohio 44313
Pony	13–14	Boys Baseball, Inc. Box 225 Washington, Pennsylvania 15301
Professional	Adult	National Baseball Congress Box 1420 Wichita, Kansas 62201
Professional	Adult	The Sporting News 1212 N. Lindbergh Blvd. St. Louis, Missouri 63166
Sandy Koufax	14 and under	American Amateur Baseball Congress Box 5332 Akron, Ohio 44313
Semi-Pro	No age limit	National Baseball Congress Box 1420 Wichita, Kansas 62201
Stan Musial	No age limit	American Amateur Baseball Congress Box 5332 Akron, Ohio 44313
Y.M.C.A.		Contact the local Y.M.C.A. in your community.

LINGO

Ace	A team's best pitcher
Blue Darter	A line drive through the infield
Boner	Mental mistake
Chinese Home Run	A short, or wind-blown, home run
Clubhouse Lawyer	A player who carries on constantly, as if he knows it all
Cousin	A pitcher who is easy for a certain batter is referred to as that batter's cousin
Fireman	Relief pitcher
Goat	The player who made the mistake that lost the game
Gopher Ball	A home-run pitch
Grapefruit League	The exhibition games played during spring training
Handcuffed Him	Said of an infielder when a ball gets through him, because it was too hot to handle
Horse Collar	Used to indicate going hitless in a game—the player wore the collar
In the Hole	The player who is two places away from coming to bat is in the hole; or, between 3rd and short
Iron Man	A pitcher who can pitch constantly and never seems to tire
Nightcap	The last game of a doubleheader
On Deck	The player who follows the batter in the batting order is on deck
Rabbit Ears	A player who is easily disturbed by the fans' or opposing team's comments has rabbit ears
Rhubarb	A heated argument on the field involving the manager, umpire, and several players
Scratch Hit	Poorly hit ball topped or blooped for a base hit
Skipper	The manager
South Paw	A left-handed pitcher
Tee Off	When the batter takes a full swing against a weak pitcher or against a pitcher who has tired and the result is a long hit ball, he has teed off
Texas Leaguer	Short fly ball base hit between the infield and outfield
Tools of Ignorance	The catcher's equipment
Two O'Clock Hitter	A player who hits well in batting practice, but can't hit in the game (major league games used to start at three o'clock)
Whitewashing	A team that scored no runs during the game received a whitewashing

AVERAGES AND PERCENTAGES

BATTING AVERAGE

Divide the number of official times at bat into the number of hits.

Example:
63—at bats
20—hits

```
        .317
63)20.000   Add 3 zeros
   18 9
   ────
   1 10
     63
   ────
    470
    441
   ────
    29/63
```

A base on balls or sacrifice out does not count as an official "at bat."

EARNED RUN AVERAGE

Divide the number of innings pitched into 9 times the number of earned runs.

Example:
23—innings pitched
8—earned runs
(8 x 9 = 72)

```
        3.13
23)72.00    Add 2 zeros
   69
   ──
   3 0
   2 3
   ───
    70
    69
   ──
    1/23
```

When you have a fractional number of innings pitched, you either drop ⅓ or add ⅓ to make a whole number (21⅓ becomes 21; 21⅔ becomes 22).

FIELDING PERCENTAGE

Divide total chances into assists + putouts.
Total chances are assists + putouts + errors.

Example:

Assists   12
Putouts   8
          ───
           20
Errors   3
          ───
           23 Total chances

```
         .869
23)20.000    Add 3 zeros
   18 4
   ────
   1 60
   1 38
   ────
    220
    207
   ────
    13/23
```

SLUGGING PERCENTAGE

Divide the number of official times at bat into the total number of bases.

Example

At Bats	Total Bases
(1) Single	1
(2) Out	0
(3) Out	0
(4) Double	2
(5) Out	0
(6) Out	0
(7) Home run	4
(8) Out	0
	7

At Bats—8
Total Bases—7

$$\begin{array}{r} .875 \\ 8\overline{)7.000} \quad \text{Add 3 zeros} \\ 6\,4 \\ \hline 60 \\ 56 \\ \hline 40 \\ 40 \\ \hline \end{array}$$

A base on balls or a sacrifice out does not count as an official time at bat.

RECORDS

Hitting	Season			Lifetime	
		Record	Year		
At Bats	Willie Wilson	705	1980	Pete Rose	14,053
Strikeouts	Bobby Bonds	189	1970	Reggie Jackson	2,597
Bases on Balls	Babe Ruth	170	1923	Babe Ruth	2,056
Doubles	Earl Webb	67	1931	Tris Speaker	793
Triples	Owen Wilson	36	1912	Sam Crawford	312
Home Runs	Roger Maris	61	1961	Hank Aaron	755
Hits	George Sisler	257	1920	Pete Rose	4,256
Pinch Hits	Jose Morales	25	1976	Manny Mota	150
Extra-Base Hits	Babe Ruth	119	1921	Hank Aaron	1,429
Total Bases	Babe Ruth	457	1921	Hank Aaron	6,591
Runs Batted In	Hack Wilson	190	1930	Babe Ruth	2,217
Stolen Bases	Rickey Henderson	130	1982	Ty Cobb	892
Runs Scored	Billy Hamilton	196	1894	Ty Cobb	2,245
Batting Average	Hugh Duffy	.438	1894	Ty Cobb	.367

Pitching					
Games	Mike Marshall	106	1974	Hoyt Wilhelm	1,070
Games Started	Amos Rusie	52	1893	Cy Young	816
Games Completed	Amos Rusie	50	1893	Cy Young	756
Innings Pitched	Amos Ruise	482	1893	Cy Young	7,356
Strikeouts	Nolan Ryan	383	1973	Nolan Ryan	5,308
Bases on Balls	Amos Rusie	218	1893	Nolan Ryan	2,540
Earned Run Average	Dutch Leonard	1.01	1914	Ed Walsh	1.82
Shutouts	Grover Alexander	16	1916	Walter Johnson	110
Wins	Jack Chesbro	41	1904	Cy Young	511
Saves	Bobby Thigpen	57	1990	Rollie Fingers	341
Losses	Red Donahue	35	1897	Cy Young	315
Winning Percentage	Roy Face	.947	1959	Bob Caruthers	.692

INDEX